THE MANNERS AND CUSTOMS
OF THE CHINESE

THE

MANNERS AND CUSTOMS

OF THE

CHINESE

BY

J. D. VAUGHAN

WITH AN INTRODUCTION BY
WILFRED BLYTHE

SINGAPORE
OXFORD UNIVERSITY PRESS
OXFORD NEW YORK
PENERBIT FAJAR BAKTI SDN. BHD.

Oxford University Press

Oxford New York Toronto
Delhi Bombay Calcutta Madras Karachi
Petaling Jaya Singapore Hong Kong Tokyo
Nairobi Dar es Salaam Cape Town
Melbourne Auckland
and associated companies in
Berlin Ibadan

Oxford is a trade mark of Oxford University Press

Introduction © Oxford University Press Pte. Ltd., 1971
Originally published as The Manners and Customs
of the Chinese of the Straits Settlements
by the Mission Press, Singapore, 1879
Reprinted in Oxford in Asia Historical Reprints *1971*
Reissued as an Oxford University Press paperback 1974
Fourth impression 1992

ISBN 0 19 588581 3

For sale in Malaysia only

Printed in Malaysia by Peter Chong Printers Sdn. Bhd.
Published by Oxford University Press Pte. Ltd.,
Unit 221, Ubi Avenue 4, Singapore 1440

INTRODUCTION

JONAS Daniel Vaughan, like many another who served the government of the Straits Settlements in the nineteenth century, spent his early life at sea. Born on 27 June 1825, he served as a midshipman in the East India Company's frigate *Tenasserim*, and his first glimpse of Singapore was in 1842 *en route* to participate in the final stages of the 'Opium War' in China. From 1846 he served on the Straits station in the armed steamers *Phlegathon* and *Nemesis* and set himself to study the Malay language. This led to his appointment as First Officer in the government vessel *Hooghly*. In 1851 he was appointed to the post of Superintendent of Police, Penang, where he remained until 1856. Thereafter he was the Master Attendant at Singapore until 1861 when he was appointed to be the Police Magistrate and later he officiated as Assistant Resident, Singapore. In 1869 while in England on leave he qualified as a barrister of the Middle Temple, and on his return to Singapore in that year resigned from government service to set up as an advocate and solicitor, in which profession he continued until his death in 1891. He was lost overboard from s.s. *Malacca* while returning from a visit to one of his married daughters at Alor Gajah, Malacca.[1]

In all, then, Vaughan lived permanently in the Straits Settlements for forty-five years, and it is clear that his five or six years in Penang brought him into close contact with the Chinese community there. It was in 1845 that his 'Notes on the Chinese of Pinang' which forms the kernel of the present book appeared anonymously in J.R. Logan's *Journal of the Indian Archipelago* Vol. VII. From his frequent references to the work of Davis on the Chinese we may infer that he was familiar with *The Chinese, a general Description of the Empire of China and its Inhabitants*, by John Francis Davis, first published in 1836.

No one would regard Vaughan as a literary stylist. His book is an ill-arranged hotchpotch of things seen and heard, but he had a keenness of observation and enquiry and an evident urge to set down all that he

---

[1] Details from an article in the *Sunday Times* (*Singapore*) 23 June 1957.

had learned concerning the customs and behaviour of the Chinese communities in the Straits. As with most Western writers of his time, this behaviour was measured against Western concepts of ethics and convention, but though at times he was led to unfavourable generalizations —as in his description of the Chinese at page 43: ('. . . . crafty, proud conceited, treacherous . . .') it is noteworthy that this was in juxtaposition to a catalogue of their virtues ('sober, industrious, domesticated, methodical . . .'). Allowing for the general conviction of superiority displayed by most Western writers of the time when faced with the seemingly strange manifestations of other civilizations, it is, I think, fair to say that Vaughan's outlook was tempered with respect and appreciation. But leaving aside the question of prejudicial assessment, the value of his book from the standpoint of history and social anthropology lies in the facts it records. Incomplete though these are, they do enable us to form some idea of the life of the Chinese in the Straits in Vaughan's day, a background against which to evaluate social changes which have since taken place whilst recognizing some of the features which still persist.

Without commenting in detail on his conclusions, one may, perhaps, draw attention to his somewhat equivocal attitude to secret societies. At pages 98-101 he disagrees with Pickering's view that secret societies created far more trouble than disputes between clan or language groups, even going so far as to declare that if immigration from China were limited to men from one province there would be peace. Yet there is ample evidence from China, from Hong Kong, and from Malaya that bitter fighting has occurred between men from the same province. It is true that wherever one society and one alone existed that society could enforce its control for it had complete power of discipline and punishment; it was in effect the government. But, as Vaughan rightly adds, 'unfortunately, from the original society splitting up into a dozen rival societies more elements of discord, it is true, are introduced.' And this is what repeatedly happened. Furthermore, at page 112, he is constrained to remark, 'One of the greatest objections the writer can urge against the secret societies is that it gives the headmen of unscrupulous characters the opportunity of establishing a reign of terror among the people'. Quite so.

Finally, one may remark upon a common error: that of regarding the Chinese as a homogeneous ethnic group with a pattern of culture common to all its members. There are, it is true, common factors just as there are between different peoples of Europe, but there are also very considerable differences when we come to examine specific items such as the ceremonies performed on betrothal, at marriage, at death and on other occasions. Vaughan frequently treats 'the Chinese' as a group, but he was sufficiently observant to notice that differences did exist and to record, after describing some rite, that the Hokkiens varied from the Cantonese or that Tiechiu practice differed from Hokkien. Unfortunately, the extent of these variations is not fully revealed and we must content ourselves with the facts as stated.

And here, it seems to me, lies a field for research to which more attention might well be paid. It is a field best worked, I suggest, by students whose parents were born in China and still retain full knowledge of the customs of their territorial groups, students who are themselves of the particular group, speaking its sub-dialect and able to hear and observe with full understanding. A series of studies of this nature would provide a remarkable fund of detailed knowledge for the furtherance of sociological investigation.

If the reprint of Vaughan's book should encourage an urge in this direction it will have been well worth while.

Jersey   WILFRED BLYTHE
Channel Islands
April 1970

PUBLISHER'S NOTE

It is regrettable that the elegant (and rare) first edition, printed at the Mission Press, Singapore in 1879, could not be photographically reproduced for this edition. This was not possible because the only copy available to the Publisher was too faded and too much marked. The type therefore had to be reset. Literals and inconsistencies in spelling have been corrected but not stylistic oddities.

PREFACE

THE following notes upon the Chinese of the Straits Settlements are based upon a paper I wrote on the Chinese of Penang in 1854 which was published by the late MR. JAMES RICHARDSON LOGAN in his Journal of the Indian Archipelago. Much more might be written on the subject, and I am sensible of my short-comings in a literary point of view; but I trust my notes, though crude and unartistically put together may convince the reader that, the Chinese of this Colony are a superior race and worthy of all encouragement by our Government so long as the indulgences accorded to them do not infringe on the liberties or comfort of their fellow citizens. In writing this book I have derived many hints from the pages of DAVIS, LOGAN, and CRAWFURD.

J. D. VAUGHAN

THE

MANNERS AND CUSTOMS

OF THE CHINESE

OF THE STRAITS SETTLEMENTS

———

The manners and customs of the Chinese of the Straits Settlements, chiefly those born in the Colony called *Babas,* are briefly portrayed in the following pages. Of the numerous races settled in this Colony the Chinese attract the greatest attention. It is no exaggeration to say, that to these to a great extent, may be attributed the wonderful progress and prosperity of Singapore. MR. CRAWFURD who was Governor of this Settlement in 1823, only four years after we took possession of the island, wrote in a dispatch to the Government of India that, he estimated the worth of one Chinaman to the State as equal to two Klings or four Malays; and an experience of nearly sixty years has confirmed his valuation.

We have in this Colony at present about 200,000 Malays; 20,000 Klings; and 150,000 Chinese. The first have remained nearly stationary, so far as their occupations are concerned; we found them fishermen and paddy planters when we came amongst them and they remain so to the present day. Not a single Malay can be pointed out as having raised himself by perseverance and diligence, as a merchant or otherwise, to a prominent position in the Colony. The Klings, natives of the Coromandel coast, are an active, industrious race it is true; but neither of them can it be said that any of them has risen to any distinction but they seem content to plod on as boatmen, hack syces, and petty shopkeepers. Not a single wealthy Kling can be pointed out. The Chitties are not included in these remarks; they may be regarded as mere visitors, who have the command of fabulous sums of money it is true, but are not, as a rule, rich individually. They are generally agents of wealthy men at Madras; they take very little interest in the Colony and hasten back again to their own country as quickly as they can.

But when we turn to the Chinese what a striking contrast is presented; for the most part they are permanent residents and identify themselves with the interests of the Colony. They are the most active, industrious, and persevering of all. They equal or surpass the Europeans in developing the resources of the Colony in particular and the Indian Archipelago in general. Many have amassed large fortunes, and raised themselves high in the estimation of their fellow citizens; and one, the Honourable MR. WHAMPOA, has reached the zenith of the aspirations of all loyal citizens, a seat in the Legislative Council of the Colony and a Companionship in the exalted order of St. Michael and St. George; and it is hoped that his example, which sheds a lustre upon his countrymen, may not be lost upon him.

The Chinese born in the Straits are called *Babas* to distinguish them from those born in China. The term *Baba* is used by the natives of Bengal to designate the children of Europeans and it is probable that the word was applied by the Indian convicts at Pinang to Chinese children and so came into general use. The word *Baba* is given in Douglas's Hokien dictionary as meaning a half-caste Chinese from the Straits. In the Straits however the term is applied to all Chinese born there, half-caste or otherwise.

The Chinese are so attached to the habits of their forefathers, that notwithstanding an intercourse in the Straits for many generations with natives of all countries they have zealously adhered to their ancient manners and customs. The intercourse has been so long and so intimate that the Chinese have indelibly impressed their type ethnologically speaking upon the native inhabitants of the Colony to a great extent; as well as upon the descendants of Portuguese, Dutch, and English of mixed breed. In many persons of both sexes to be met with in the Straits, with fair complexions and auburn or reddish hair, may be seen the oblique narrow eyes, and other unmistakable indications of their Mongolian descent.

One may see in Malacca *Babas* who can claim no connection with China for centuries, clad in long jackets, loose drawers, and black skull caps, the very counterparts of Chinese to be seen any day at Amoy, Chusan, or under the walls of Nankin. Strange to say that although the *Babas* adhere so loyally to the customs of their progenitors they despise the real Chinaman and are exclusive fellows indeed; nothing they rejoice in more than being British subjects. The writer has seen *Babas* on being asked if they were Chinamen bristle up and say in an offended tone "I am not a Chinaman, I am a British subject, an *Orang putih*" literally, a white man; this term is invariably applied to an Englishman. They have social clubs of their own to which they will admit no native of China. At these clubs they play at billiards, bowls, and other European games, and drink brandy and soda *ad libitum;* yet they adhere strictly to the Chinese costume—the queue, thick soled shoes, mandarin dresses, and conical hats on state occasions, and the manners and customs of those people who otherwise they have no sympathies with. The Duke of Edinburgh when in Singapore in 1869, visited a Chinese Club and bowled with the *Babas* and expressed himself highly pleased with their pluck. The true Chinaman ridicules the idea of exercise in any shape. The use of tobacco is universal amongst the Chinese.

It is well known to the *Baba* that the queue is a badge of servitude; that it was imposed upon the Chinese by their Manchu conquerors and that there is a strict law in China that the natives must shave their heads and wear tails, and not wear their hair loose and flowing according to ancient custom, except at death, when it may be combed out in the style of their ancestors. One of the first innovations introduced by the leader of the "Tai Ping" rebellion in China, was to cut off the queue and allow the hair to grow all over the head as the Chinese did under the rule of their native Emperors. One would imagine that the *Babas,* and the natives of China themselves, when they got away from the thraldom of their Tartar rulers, would glady avail themselves of their liberty and discard their queues, but such is not the case; you can offer no greater insult to a *Baba* than to cut his tail off, or even to threaten to do so. In our criminal prisons tails are shorn off the worst class of Chinese prisoners. This punishment is felt keenly at the time, but is easily remedied on the convict's release by the skilful barber, who will fix on with very little trouble a handsome queue to the baldest cranium. It is not an uncommon occurrence for the tail of a Chinese thief to slip off on being seized by a policeman, leaving so little hair on the head that one wonders how the false tail was fastened on. Many Chinese are converted to Christianity in the Straits but in no instance have they abandoned their queues and national costume in consequence.

The *Baba* as a rule has no desire to visit China; he does not regard it as his home, as the descendants of Englishmen do the old country whereever they may be born. In Malacca the Chinese were found when the

Portuguese first made their appearance in these waters more than three hundred years ago, and they have been permanently settled there for many generations; and in Penang and Singapore they have been settled ninety and sixty years respectively, and yet they remain unchanged. One custom however has been entirely abandoned, viz., the barbarous practice of crushing the feet of girls and making them small-footed.

The Hindu and Mahomedan settlers from India in the Straits soon lay aside caste prejudices, and much of their distinctiveness. The writer has known them to subscribe indiscriminately to a Musjid in Penang consecrated to the memory of a Mahomedan Saint, and they imitate each other as well as the Chinese on their holy-days by firing crackers and beating gongs. Mussalmen may be seen seated in the houses of ortho-dox Hindus eating off the same board; and the Hindu has no hesitation in cohabiting with Mahomedan women. Such a proceeding in India would render them outcasts for ever, but here they do not lose caste. The writer has seen a Hindu and a Muslim bathing in the same tank, the water from the latter's body falling on the former and *vice versa*. Such a sight in India would be a novelty indeed. There the educated native, especially if converted to Christianity, apes the manners and costume of the European; but the Chinese with characteristic obstinacy and hard-headedness eschew everything European. Some who have all their lives *feted* Europeans and lived on the most intimate terms with them, have sent their sons to England to be educated, letting them cut off their tails whilst there and assume the European garb, and attend the services of our church and profess Christianity, have on the return of the latter to the Straits ruthlessly forced them back to the old order of things — the Chinese costume and the worship of idols; nor do the fathers in spite of their life-long intimacy with Europeans and their outward display of a leaning towards them, abate one jot in all their superstitious and heathenish observances. This conduct is a fearful commentary upon the boasted superiority of our institutions.

The real Chinaman respects his tail, but is not so sensitive about it as the *Baba*. Some of the former, converts to Mahomedanism, cut off their queues, assume the Malay attire and identify themselves in every parti-cular with their adopted brethren. Very few half-caste Chinese having Malay mothers, adopt the Mahomedan religion or costume, but faith-fully follow their father's example in everything. Even when the fathers die leaving the children young and entirely under the mother's control, the women bring them up as Chinese. It is striking sometimes to see very black Chinese with all the characteristics of their fathers strongly brought out. In Malacca where the Malays are in the majority, the women are more prejudiced and lean more to their own people.

But to return to my subject: The Chinaman on first landing in the Straits is called a Sinkeh, meaning a new man or new friend. The term is used generally by all classes. Immigrants from China are chiefly from Canton, and its neighbourhood; Swatow, and the island of Hainan all in the province of Quantung; and from Amoy and other places in the province of Fuhkeen; maritime provinces and said to be the most turbulent in China, and consist of fishermen, pirates, artisans and laborers, the poorest of the poor. SIR JOHN DAVIS says in his work on China, 'There is a peculiar turbulence about the character of the people on the sea coast of this province Quantung, as well as the adjoining one of Fuhkeen, which distinguishes them from other Chinese, and has been frequently noticed in the Government proclamations, especially in regard to the spirit of clanship which is a frequent source of so much disorder. This difference may be perhaps attributed to the seafaring habits which distinguish them from the rest of the Empire. The most notorious place for these excesses is the district of Chaou-Chaou on the frontiers of Canton and Fuhkeen but still in the former province. One of the inhabitants some years since carried his appeal even to Pekin against the magistrates, who either would not or could not, restrain the outrages. His kindred having refused to assist two other clans in that neighborhood to fight in their feuds, suffered the most shocking cruelties in consequence. Their houses were laid in ruins; several hundred acres of land seized and devastated; money plundered; temples of ancestors thrown down; graves dug up; and the water cut off from the rice fields. Many persons were killed; more still were maimed, and crippled for life, and notwithstanding the large reward offered for the apprehension of the leaders, such was the organization which bound them together that they escaped unpunished. The immense fleets of pirates who have often continued for years to infest the southern coasts, may partly account for the existence of a maritime population in these two provinces distinguished by a ferocity of character so different from the peaceful mildness of the other Chinese.' One need scarcely be surprised with such a population at the outbreaks that have occurred so frequently in

[5]

the Straits between the natives of these two provinces; the only wonder is that the Colony is so peaceful as it is. The outrages so graphically described by DAVIS were enacted to the very letter in the riots of 1854 in Singapore which occurred between the Cantonese and Hokiens, and were not suppressed until the island was placed under martial law. The speedy appearance of the military in 1871 when a riot broke out between the same people, has tended much to restrain the turbulent disposition of the unruly inhabitants.

None of the middle or upper classes nor women emigrate. There is no law in China prohibiting the emigration of women, or any particular class, but there is a reluctance on the part of the Chinese to quit their native country, and it is only dire necessity that compels the poor to do so. Of late years many women have come down, chiefly prostitutes, who are brought by brothel keepers to carry on their trade here. The writer knows no instance of a respectable woman emigrating with her husband. The wealthy Chinese go to China for wives but these can scarcely be called emigrants. In the Straits the Chinese are classed under five heads, *Macaos*, natives of Canton and neighbouring towns and villages; *Kehs* from the interior of the province of Quantung; *Tay Chews* from Swatow and its vicinity; *Hylams*, natives of the island of Hainan; and *Hokiens* from Amoy and other places in the province of Fuhkeen; very few emigrants come from the other provinces of China. The writer has however met a few, even Mahomedans from one of the western provinces.

The immigrants are thus obtained: A number of Chinese familiar with the Straits collect them in China by holding out prospects of a speedy fortune and quick return to their native land and bring them down in junks, sailing vessels, or steamers, and dispose of them to the residents to the best advantage, the immigrants mortgaging their labor for twelve months to repay their passage money. This cooly trade as it is called was once exceedingly remunerative. It used to be an animating sight to see the arrival of junks in the Straits during the N.E. Monsoon laden with Sinkehs. Hundreds of shoe boats hastened off with residents anxious to *buy*, as they called it, the new arrivals. They climbed up the junks' sides and inspected the passengers attentively, selecting the healthiest looking fellows, for whom they paid a certain sum to the trader; a fixed sum was placed on each man sufficiently remunerative to cover all expenses, leaving a good margin for the benefit of the speculator. Sometimes the coolies were disposed of according to their qualifications;

[6]

a master workman fetching a high price, a laborer something less, and a sickly man a few dollars. The Sinkeh during his probation received from his purchaser food, clothes, and a few dollars for remittance to his family in China. The immigrants were detained on board until disposed of; or sometimes were landed and detained in houses hired for the purpose. The police interfered occasionally, setting the coolies free, on the ground that they were illegally detained, causing much loss to the traders. The system of immigration above described prevailed ever since Pinang and Singapore were taken possession of by us; and during an experience of thirty years the writer knows no instance of immigrants suffering in consequence; and the Chinese themselves were perfectly satisfied.

The local Government however has lately at great expense established a Protectorate of the Chinese, with the approbation of some influential Chinese, and appointed in the month of May 1877 two gentlemen, the one a well known Chinese scholar, and the other reputed to possess an exceptionally good acquaintance with cooly-trade matters, MESSRS. PICKERING and DENNYS, Protectors of Chinese. Before this step was taken the cooly trade had nearly disappeared.

Several steamers now ply regularly between the Straits and ports in China and convey coolies to and fro at very moderate charges; the coolies themselves having learnt to a great extent to do without the intervention of middle-men; since the establishment of the Protectorate all junks arriving in Singapore are required to report to the Protectorate and the strictest vigilance is exercised to prevent an overcharge being made for passage money and advances. Up to the end of April 1878 nearly forty thousand immigrants have come under the control of the Protectorate, and no dissatisfaction has been expressed by the Chinese community. The Sinkeh still however mortgages his labor to the person who takes him over through the Protectorate, to repay the money advanced for passage money and other expenses. The writer is of opinion that, the directing powers of Europeans brought to bear upon the Chinese at their first entrance into the Straits through the instrumentality of the Protectorate, will serve more effectually to destroy the baneful influences of the secret societies than any means that could have been devised. Branches of the Protectorate are being established at Pinang and Malacca. Many thousand immigrants annually land at the several ports of the Colony, and spread themselves over the adjoining Native

States. During each year thousands return to China, leaving the fixed Chinese population in the Straits somewhat stationary.

From the absence of females the increase of the Chinese population by natural means is very slow. Female immigration should be encouraged by our Government to prevent, if for no other reason, the fearful crimes that prevail amongst the Chinese in consequence of the paucity of females. They exceed all belief and may not be placed in all their repulsiveness before the public. The introduction of women would materially conduce to the peacefulness of the Colony. The Chinese are naturally domesticated, and would, surrounded by their wives and children seek to maintain order and peace; and would not be easily roused as they now are with no ties to restrain them, to side with one faction or another in the event of a quarrel taking place between them. The bulk of the Chinese women now in the Colony are purchased in China from their parents by bawds and panders, and have to repay their purchase money and other advances by prostituting their bodies, for years it may be. The lives of slavery and debauchery these poor creatures lead, ending often in disease and death, is something horrible to contemplate. They are somewhat protected by the Contagious Diseases Ordinance, and the writer can bear witness to the untiring exertions of the gentlemen appointed by Government to carry the provisions of that ordinance into effect (Mr. Cousins the Registrar General, and Messrs. Phillips and Cooper his assistants) to get these women free and encourage them to lead pure and virtuous lives; many have through their influence left the brothels and married, and are happy and contented.

The streets of Singapore at this day present a striking contrast to what they did a quarter of a century ago, so far as the presence of women is concerned. In 1856, when the writer came to Singapore as a permanent resident, there was on the island but one Chinese woman to eighteen or nineteen men, and a Chinese woman was seldom seen out of doors. Now, dozens may be met at every turning, trudging along to market, or sauntering about with their children, or shopping, or driving in omnibuses and hack carriages. The inequality of the sexes has been reduced, but is still sufficient to account for the immorality that prevails. The population of this Colony is of the most heterogeneous nature. It embraces eight and twenty or more nationalities, the Chinese forming more than a third of the whole, there being about one hundred and fifty thousand or more in the three settlements.

The remittance of money to poor relations in China is a duty most religiously observed by the Chinese, so long as there is any one left there that needs support. Confucius enjoined the love and care of parents as one of the chief duties of man; and the laws of China enforce the precept; and to the honor of the Chinese be it said the law is strictly obeyed. One never hears instances of parents being neglected by their children in the Straits. The poorest Sinkeh manages to scrape together a dollar or two during the year for his poor folk at home, which he remits through Chinese bankers who faithfully deliver these remittances to the addressees in the remotest parts of Fuhkeen and Quantung. The Colonial Government undertook this service a short time ago, by taking some of the native bankers into their service as postmasters; but the scheme proved unpopular and resulted in utter failure. The bulk of the Chinese set themselves against the innovation; a riot broke out which was speedily repressed by the police firing at and killing some of the rioters; a proceeding that is likely to have the most salutary effect on the Chinese population. The Government Chinese Post Office and money order system has been closed; the Chinese contractors having suffered a heavy loss.

At the end of twelve months the immigrant is a free man, and he may enter his master's service on a monthly salary or seek his livelihood elsewhere. The attire of the Sinkeh is exceedingly light and economical. It consists simply of a pair of short drawers tied round the waist by a dirty piece of string, and his feet are sometimes protected by a pair of straw sandals. He gets his food at the itinerant kitchens and soup stalls for a few cents a day; a good substantial meal consisting of a stew of pork and vegetables may be bought for two cents; and he lodges at cooly houses for a trifle. He wears red thread twisted up in his tail with a tassel of same color at the end when he can afford it, and as he advances in years exchanges red thread for black; red in the tail is essentially a Straits custom; Doctor Dennys informs the writer that red is worn in China by children only. A false tail is often added to the real made of thread or silk, making the whole queue of considerable length and thickness, which becomes a formidable weapon of offence in street rows.

The Sinkeh ekes out his livelihood by carrying loads, coaling steamers, or doing any odd jobs that he may pick up in the streets, and earns ten or twenty cents a day or more if robust and active; after the labors of the day he adjourns to one of the open air theatres and witnesses the performance free of expense; or spends the evening at his lodgings playing at cards or dominoes or other games staking a few cents to give the pastime a zest. He is often arrested by the police and fined by the Magistrate for playing in a common gaming house when he has been legally enjoying a game at his lodgings with none but the inmates. Wealthy gamesters in the meanwhile escape with impunity being able to elude the vigilance of the police by playing in out-of-the-way places, or at the houses of wealthy persons who are above suspicion, or by greasing the palms of the police to allow them to play unmolested. To the short trowsers the Sinkeh adds a leaf conical hat should he take to a rural life as a cooly on a pepper or gambier plantation. Boatmen and fishermen indulge in no more clothing. The former reside for years in their boats in which they carry their all and never sleep ashore; never marry; know none of the pleasures of social or domestic life, and yet seem happy and contented.

The condition of the poor man in this colony is exceedingly happy—he requires little clothing and very little money to make him comfortable.

They have boats of all sizes built on the model of the well known Chinese junk. The smallest are used for carrying passengers and are called shoe boats; and are propelled by one man who stands facing the prow of the boat; the oars are suspended with a loop on a strong peg at the side of the boat: when under sail and the oars are not used they are let go, when they swing to the side of the boat and do not impede her way. The larger boats for carrying cargo are called *Toah-koh* and are manned by two, three, or more men, according to their size. All these boats are propelled by a single scull at the stern worked sometimes by ten or fifteen men upon the principle of a steamer's screw. Each boat has an eye painted on each bow for John Chinaman says "no got eye how can see, no can see how can sabee."†

The fishing boats are built on a different model. They are long and narrow rising at each end high out of the water with something of a keel which the junk class of boats have not. They are rowed by eight or ten men in European fashion and are very fast. They use long narrow nets with floats on the upper edge, and weights on the lower to keep them

---

† This however is a joke formerly played off on "griffins" in China; the marks in question are not eyes, but charms, *Dr.—Dennys*

upright which are run out athwart the tide so as to enclose the fish brought down by the stream. The waters of the Straits swarm with fish and the market is plentifully supplied by Chinese fishermen. Besides these seine nets the Chinese fish with casting nets, and nets fixed to stakes, but never with lines and hooks. The capital required to purchase fishing boats and nets is advanced by town fishmongers to whom all the fish has to be delivered at certain prices fixed on between the fishermen and the capitalist.

The clothing of a Chinaman whatever his rank in life may be, differs little from the description above given of the dress of a Sinkeh. Add to the trowsers a long jacket or coat called a *Baju*, and a pair of thick soled shoes, and you have the toilet of a gentleman. The swell *Baba* rejoices sometimes in patent leather shoes and a felt or straw hat; but as a rule the dress of a Chinaman is exceedingly simple and economical and well adapted to the exigencies of the climate. The ordinary bed of a Chinaman consists of a few planks placed upon trestles covered over with a mat, with a hard wooden or bamboo pillow for his head.

The rich indulge in mattresses, and handsome massive bedsteads covered with ornamental hangings, but seldom use soft pillows for the head. Women from China wear the *baju* and drawers also, and dress the hair in most fantastic devices, and paint the face white and red. The Straits China women wear the Malay *Cabayah* and *Sarong*, the former fastened with brooches of various shapes often set with precious stones. The hair is tied in a knot at the back of the head held together by hair-pins of silver and gold, richly ornamented. These women when young are pretty and graceful, but want of exercise soon renders them obese and unwieldly; and after bearing a few children they degenerate in-to ugly hags. Nothing can be more ungainly than the waddling gait of a middle aged female *Baba*. The women from China usually wear thick wooden clogs; but *Babas* indulge in pretty worked slippers and the ordinary shaped European leather shoes. The habit of smoking tobacco is not confined to men. Chinese women smoke it in brass pipes and rolled up in paper as cigarettes, and some take to opium like their lords and masters. Opium smoking amongst women however is confined to a limited circle and the Straits-born Chinese women do

---

Baju a coat, upper garment or jerkin, *Crawfurd.*
Cabaya, a loose robe or dressing gown, *Crawfurd.*
Sarong, a sheath; the body clothes or main part of dress consisting of a single piece of cloth wrapped round the lower part of the person, *Crawfurd.*

not as a rule indulge in tobacco; a young lady that smoked would be looked upon as decidedly fast.

Every Chinaman must shave the greater part of his head, and barbers abound in consequence and carry on a thriving trade; in every village some may be found. Besides these there is a vast number of itinerant barbers who are always tramping about the country plying their trade. Their razors are triangular in shape and awkward looking but are exceedingly sharp, and are deftly handled by their owners. Besides shaving materials the barber carries a number of sharp pointed picks and pincers for picking and cleaning the ears, and removing any stray hairs that may make their appearance on the face before their allotted time. The writer on one occasion overhauled a travelling barber's box and found in it five triangular razors; one small narrow razor about the size of a penknife used for shaving the ears and eyelids; three strong combs, and half a dozen earpicks. The price for shaving ranges from seven to ten cents. Once a week the tail has to be opened out combed thoroughly and replaited with fresh silk if necessary. The fop rather prides himself on the gay color of his tassel which is usually a bright red. Blue and white are mourning colors. Black is usually worn in old age. The shaven part of the head is also well scrubbed with soap and water once a week. The barber goes quickly over the head and every part of the face, even the eyelids, and in half an hour turns his man out looking clean and fresh.

The earpicking seems to affect the hearing of nearly all Chinese. It is no easy task to get them to hear you in the streets when driving, and many accidents occur apparently through the deafness of the foot passengers. In every barber's shop may be seen at any time of the day two or three men undergoing the operation of shaving, earpicking, and shampooing; every appliance is neatly arranged and conveniently placed for the use of the barber and his assistants. The travelling barber, carries a small box containing his razors and other tools slung at one end of a pole, on the other he has a stand, basin and napkins.

The use of the umbrella is general. The poorest cooly manages to scrape money enough together to buy one made either of paper or cotton. In the country roads hundreds of Chinese may be seen trudging along with umbrellas spread, although it may be cloudy weather and not a vestige of the sun to be seen. Late in the evening too the umbrella is carefully kept open and held over the head. The height of respectability appears to be a clean white baju and silk umbrella. The writer has often been amused to see a well known low fellow step into the witness box of a court with his umbrella and white baju, borrowed doubtless, to impress the lookers on with his respectability; the fan is also indispensable.

Many Sinkehs find employment in husking rice in riceshops as well as for private families. The grain is placed in large stone mortars, and is pounded by pestles fixed to horizontal levers which are balanced on a pivot. The cooly stands at the end of the lever and presses the end down with his foot raising the pestle as high as it will go and then removing his foot and letting the pestle fall into the mortar. After sufficient pounding the rice is removed from the mortar and a fresh supply put in.

There are many rice mills in which wheels are moved by water turning cylinders to whose circumference are attached cams which meeting the extremeties of the levers, strike them down alternately, and raise the pestles at the other end just as is done in China and described by SIR JOHN DAVIS in his work on the Chinese. There are also upright pounders in these mills worked by the cams. In a few mills steam has been substituted for water power, to the benefit of the owners who derive considerable profit from these mills.

It is very amusing to see the coolies working at the mortars. They stand in a row working away at the levers all day drenched in perspiration, each armed with a leaf fan, which he works with all his might to keep himself cool,— a difficult task in the heated atmosphere of a small room, badly ventilated and filled with the fine powder of the rice thrown up out of the mortars. The Sinkehs heed this not but chat away with each other as merry as grigs. In Singapore very little rice is cultivated but in Malacca and Province Wellesley large quantities are produced. The Chinese thresh the paddy with flails and have winnowing machines like ours. DAVIS states that we borrowed this machine from the Chinese. The Malay adopts a very ingenious mode of winnowing. The threshed paddy is taken up to a high scaffolding from which it is poured down upon clean mats spread below; the husk is blown away by the wind and the clean rice falls on the mats.

Another source of living is by hatching ducks' eggs artificially—the owner of the eggs brings them to the hatcher and pays comparatively a trifle, about a dollar and a half for one hundred ducklings that he gets back. It takes twenty seven days to hatch an egg. The eggs are placed in coarse napkins about thirty in each and deposited in layers in baskets about three feet deep. No artificial heat is used beyond the heat of the hut caused by the burning rays of the sun falling on the thatched roof which is not far from the baskets, some times paddy husk is placed with the eggs to increase the heat. As soon as the eggs are hatched the ducklings are put into a yard with plenty of water for them to dabble in. The owners of the eggs come in from all parts of the country to take them away; they find it more convenient to get their eggs hatched in this way than by the natural process; in dry weather the ducklings suffer and many die. In Egypt the writer has seen hens' eggs hatched artificially, but in every case heat was produced by burning fuel in the huts, the floors of which were strewn with eggs with chickens of various ages amongst them, some crowing with loud shrill voices.

The Sinkehs sometimes develop into wealthy fellows. If the history of the rich Chinese merchants were enquired into, it would be found that most of them landed in the Straits as poor Sinkehs. One of the richest men of his day used to boast that he landed in Singapore with nothing more than a pair of trowsers a *baju* and a mat. Canton men are more robust and hardworking than the Hokiens. All the carpenters, miners, blacksmiths, shoemakers and artisans in general come from the province of Quantung. They are excellent squatters and may be called the pioneers of the Hokiens. After completing their twelve months as Sinkehs many get an advance of money from town shopkeepers, clear a piece of forest land, plant vegetables, plantains and indigo at first, and eventually gambier and pepper; under certain government regulations forest lands are thus cleared and cultivated, and a grant obtained in perpetuity from the state. The returns are so slow, and the exactions of the money lenders so stringent, that in a few years the squatters are forced to sell their land to repay their creditors. Hokiens are often the purchasers. Most of the plantations at present in the hands of the Hokiens were cleared by Quantung men chiefly Kehs and Tay Chews. Hokiens are tailors, shopkeepers, and merchants chiefly and constitute the most wealthy portion of the Chinese inhabitants. They are great gamblers and most of the gaming houses are conducted by them. When a Cantonese contracts the habit of gambling, he is the more inveterate of the two, stakes higher and will play for all he possesses, he is looked for eagerly in the hells by the Hokiens who are cool and wary.

Tay Chews are keen traders and deal extensively in the produce of the Straits, such as gambier and pepper and amass considerable fortunes. As a rule these people yearn after China and many return as soon as they have saved money enough. They make it a point to send their children to China to be educated; not so the Hokiens, they keep their children with them and are satisfied with the education they can afford them in the Straits. The Hokien *Baba* speaks with great disparagement of the Tay Chew *Baba* educated in China; he says the Tay Chew comes back as great a *bodoh*, or simpleton, as his father and knows nothing. *Babas* speak of China amongst themselves as *Europa*.

The Chinese are everything; they are actors, acrobats, artists, musicians, chemists and druggists, clerks, cashiers, engineers, architects, surveyors, missionaries, priests, doctors, schoolmasters, lodging house keepers, butchers, porksellers, cultivators of pepper and gambier, cakesellers, cart and hackney carriage owners, cloth hawkers, distillers of spirits, eating house keepers, fishmongers, fruitsellers, ferrymen, grasssellers, hawkers, merchants and agents, oilsellers, opium shopkeepers, pawnbrokers, pig dealers, and poulterers. They are rice dealers, ship chandlers, shopkeepers, general dealers, spirit shop keepers, servants, timber dealers, tobacconists, vegetable sellers, planters, market-gardeners, laborers, bakers, millers, barbers, blacksmiths, boatmen, bookbinders, boot and shoemakers, brickmakers, carpenters, cabinet makers, carriage builders, cartwrights, cart and hackney carriage drivers, charcoal burners and sellers, coffinmakers, confectioners, contractors and builders, coopers, engine-drivers, and firemen, fishermen, goldsmiths, gunsmiths and locksmiths, limeburners, masons, and bricklayers, mat, kajang and basket makers, oil manufacturers, and miners. To which we may add painters, paper lantern makers, porters, pea grinders, printers, sago, sugar and gambier manufacturers, sawyers, seamen, ship and boat builders, soap boilers, stone cutters, sugar boilers, tailors, tanners, tinsmiths and braziers, umbrella makers, undertakers and tombbuilders, watchmakers, water carriers, wood cutters and sellers, wood tomb-builders, watchmakers, water carriers, wood cutters and sellers, wood and ivory carvers, fortune-tellers, grocers, beggars, idle vagabonds or samsengs, and thieves.

They are the most stealthy of thieves, and, it is said, stupefy their victims by burning some narcotic herb under their nostrils to increase their drowsiness, but the writer doubts the story. A petty shopkeeper in Penang was about to return to China and saved about a thousand dollars.

[15]

These he packed in paper parcels each containing fifty dollars, and placed them at the bottom of his box. To make his wealth more secure, he slept nightly on the box with the key thereof tied round his waist; on a morning or two before his intended departure he found himself lying on the floor, his box open, all the dollars gone, and the key of the box taken from his person and left in the key-hole. The door of his house had been broken open and he removed from the box, the key taken from his waist, the box opened and every dollar removed without disturbing him, or his servants who slept in an adjoining room. The writer was then in charge of the police, and disbelieved the story *in toto;* it seemed utterly incredible. Fortunately, the owner had written his name and put his chop, or seal, on each parcel of dollars which subsequently led to the detection and conviction of the thieves. Two suspicious characters had visited the shop frequently on the pretence of making purchases and had sat there each time quietly obtaining information, from the unwary shopman which served them to good purpose. The dwelling of these two men was discovered and detectives were set to watch them. It was ascertained that they were preparing also to return to China, and were making purchases and had a box or two packed ready for embarkation. On the day they were about to leave a descent was made on their shop, their boxes searched and nearly all the packets of dollars found with the prosecutor's mark name and chop intact; the thieves lodged opposite the principal police station.

On another occasion, thieves entered a bedroom in which the master of the house slept with his wife. To one of the legs of their fourposter was chained an iron safe containing their jewellery and money. The thieves entered by a window at the foot of the bed, filed the chain through, a pretty thick one, lowered the safe out of the window without disturbing the owner or his wife who slept soundly till the next morning, when they got up at the usual hour and found their wealth gone. The safe was found on the esplanade close to the Fort with the lid smashed in and contents gone; lying not far from an European sentry who had been on guard all night.

A wealthy Spanish lady at Penang was robbed of all her jewels worth several thousand dollars from a wardrobe which stood close to her bed where she lay sleeping in happy unconsciousness; the thief entered a window close to the bed. The writer had a thief come into his room at Singapore and carry off all his wife's jewels that she had placed on the dressing table close to the bed, besides other things without disturbing himself or wife. On another occasion a thief entered the writer's bedroom by a window within a foot of his bed took all his clothing and hats that were hanging on a stand not far off, as well as several things from a wardrobe; took all into the verandah selected the best hats and clothing, left the rest on the floor and decamped without disturbing any one.

Only a few months ago a lady in Singapore had a gold watch and chain taken from under her pillow whilst she and her husband lay in bed fast asleep. The Inspector General of Police also with a policeman on duty at his house was robbed of a clock and other things including a loaded revolver which hung on the tester of his bed ready for use, and neither he nor his wife were disturbed during the night; although the thief must have been a considerable time in the house and had frequently passed and repassed their bed. In many cases of house robbery there is reason to believe that the thieves are one's own servants. They sleep on the premises and often move about the house at night without exciting the suspicion of their masters, and take the opportunity some night of removing property and making it appear that thieves had entered the house.

The writer was robbed of all his plate a night or two after Christmas (1876) and in the morning it was discovered that a venetian of one of the dining room doors had been cut through to make it appear that some person had entered the house from without; but it was perfectly clear the venetian had been cut from the inside, and that it was the work of some one in the house. There was not the slightest doubt that the robbery had been committed by the servants. The property was not recovered nor was the act brought home to any of the servants.

Chinese thieves are seldom armed. One remarkable instance to the contrary came to the writer's knowledge. An old Chinaman and his wife living in the country at Singapore, finding the night warm moved their cot into the open air a few feet from the door of their house and slept. In the middle of the night they heard foot-steps inside the house which disturbed them, and shortly after they saw a man come out. The old man sprang up and seized the intruder who fired a pistol at him which did not take effect. He bravely held on assisted by the wife. A desperate struggle ensued, and at length the old man fell to the ground, but the wife held on like a tigress shrieking for help in the meantime at the top of her voice. Neighbours ran in and secured the thief. When a light was brought the husband was found stone dead with his throat cut from ear to ear; the thief was armed with a double barrelled pistol, and a long sharp knife. The murderer was hanged. His defence was ingenious: he said he had been invited to the house by the old man to gamble; that he won a considerable sum of money which the latter refused to pay, a quarrel ensued and the deceased and his wife set upon him and beat him. In self defence he used his weapons which he carried about his person to guard himself against robbers and tigers, as he had a long way to go through the jungle to reach the old man's house. On enquiry, this story was found to be utterly false; he did not reside in the country, and was well known in the town to be a bad character.

It is said that Chinese thieves are in the habit of tying fish hooks to their tails and that it is dangerous to seize the latter; the writer has known many thieves captured by their tails but never saw the latter protected by fishhooks or knives. Chinese thieves require only a pole to climb up to the highest room of a house, the pole is placed against a window and the thief walks up like a monkey and gets in. He is not quite so particular as to his exit. When chased he will spring out of a window or verandah a considerable height from the ground, fall on his feet like a cat and run off as if nothing extraordinary had happened. The writer found a thief in his verandah one pitch dark night who jumped down about twelve feet and ran headlong down a rough hill covered with large stones and boulders; a feat one could not have accomplished easily in broad daylight.

Sometimes the Chinese rob in gangs. A band of ten, twelve, or more armed to the teeth will make a sudden swoop upon the shop of a pawnbroker or licensed opium shopkeeper and in a few minutes gut the place and carry off all the money and valuables to be found in it. To accomplish their object they will take life if opposed. Robbers usually attack shops in outlying villages, but occasionally are daring enough to attack houses in the Towns. Two or three years ago a daring gang-robbery occurred in the High Street of Singapore, not far from the Government Treasury where an armed guard was stationed; the shop was plundered and owner killed. One gang robbery was actually organized in SIR HARRY ORD's stables at government house by his Chinese grooms, and some of the plunder was recovered in the royal stables. Very little stolen property is ever recovered by the police in the Straits. It is probable that it is kept concealed in the thieves' boxes in the various lodging houses about the Towns until they return to China, when they are taken off in the very sight of the police to the vessel by which the thief is returning to China.

On one occasion the writer lost some small articles of jewellery, sent for his servants and searched their persons, and in the purse of his cook found a gold ring and a gold pencil case bearing the initials and crest of a friend. On referring to the latter he said that he had been robbed of these about two years, before when the cook was in his service, and the robbery was supposed to have been committed by an out-sider and that he did not suspect his servants at the time.

On another occasion the writer was sitting writing in his drawing room when he observed a Chinese carpenter who was working in the house come out of his bed-room and descend the stairs. His suspicions were aroused and he went into the room to see if his watch was safe and found it gone. He gave chase and met the carpenter walking in at the gate looking as innocent as a child. He was seized and told that he was suspected of having taken the watch, he denied the charge indignantly and made a great noise. The writer handed him over to the mercies of his Chinese servants who were of a different race and they were told to deal with him as they pleased so long as they got the watch back. The accused was locked up in one of the out-offices and thrashed, or frightened in some way until he said if he was released, he would give up the watch; he then led the writer to the gateway and pulled out the watch from under the roots of a bamboo hedge. His intention was to have removed the watch after all search for it had been abandoned. The thief was prosecuted and punished.

They are also most ingenious smugglers of contraband *chandu*. They get tins made to fit the natural hollows of the body, such as the small of the back and the hollows of the thighs, fill them with the *chandu* which is usually prepared on some of the neighbouring islands, tie the tins on the body in their fitting places where they are safely screened by their loose attire and walk ashore as unconcernedly as possible, and often escape the vigilance of the revenue officers. On one occasion a man was seen walking along the streets of Singapore with an unusually thick pair of shoes on, the suspicions of a revenue officer, a *chinting* as he is called, was aroused, he seized the man and took him before the writer who was the Police Magistrate at the time to be examined, and in the soles of the

---

Chandu; a preparation of Opium.

shoes were found tins about an inch deep, filled with contraband *chandu*. Another dodge is to have hermetically sealed tin cases filled with *chandu* fitted into earthen jars closely, so as not to shake about, and other innocent articles are put into the jars over the tins concealing them. Smuggling is not so rife at the present time as it was a few years ago, in consequence of Hokien and Tay Chew gentlemen being interested in the Opium Farm. If the farm was sold to one race only, the other would do their utmost to smuggle contraband *chandu* into the place and ruin their rivals.

Chinese are excellent domestic servants. They are sober, industrious, methodical, and attentive to their duties. They are limited to *Macaos* and *Hylams,* and the opinion regarding the honesty of these two races is varied, some Europeans of long residence in the Straits declare *Hylam* servants to be incorrigible rogues whilst others give the same character to the *Macaos,* and prefer the *Hylams.* There are good and bad amongst both and in the writer's opinion there is little to choose between them. They are as honest as any other class of servants. Many residents give the preferance to the natives of Madras or Klings as they are called in the Straits. These invariably drink and are filthy in the extreme. The writer found a Kling cook once beating up a custard pudding with the stump of an old broom. Chinese servants will tell you that Kling cooks do all their work in the kitchen such as ornamenting or whitening cakes with their dirty fingers. A story is told of a Kling cook boiling the plum pudding in the corner of his waist cloth, who hearing his master call, rushed out of the kitchen forgetting the pudding which came flying out of the pot dangling about his heels. Chinese servants when they return to China are in the habit of lending their certificates of character to their friends who use them as their own. It is necessary therefore to have a man identified by his former master before you take him as a servant. The Chinese are exceedingly quick in learning their work.

The writer remembers some years ago taking a boy in Canton from his parents who had never been in service before. He knew nothing at first but in a few days became an exceedingly smart fellow; picked up English rapidly learnt to mend clothes and sew on buttons as if he had done so all his life; and in a very short time was the smartest servant in the fleet. He was called "Chop dollar" from the fact of his having his face pitted with small pox. Every Chinese merchant in those days put his Chop on every good dollar that passed through his hands, and the consequence was that dollars got so fearfully marked that they soon lost all traces of any design, dates or figures. Unless chopped a dollar would not be received in payment. In the Straits chopped dollars were some years ago considered the best but now they are refused, and are below par in value. Straits Chinese women do not go out to service, they are too proud to be menials.

The Sinkehs gain a livelihood also in the following way:—the towns of the Colony are without any proper system of sewage, and no underground drains exist to carry off night soil; but the latter is removed daily at early hours from the houses by Chinese gardeners, and Sinkehs who sell it to the gardeners, in pails made on a model furnished by the Police authorities, and is used to manure vegetables. It is said that the excessive use of such manure imparts an unpleasant flavour to vegetables and some Europeans will not eat them in consequence. The nightsoil is stored in pits in the vegetable gardens and is removed as required by the gardeners and poured over the plants. The country roads in the vicinity of vegetable gardens are anything but odorous thoroughfares. This manure is also used for gambier, pepper and other plants.

The streets of Singapore and the other towns in the Straits strongly resemble those of Chinese towns. The houses are narrow, seldom exceeding twenty feet in width, and the sign boards are hung out on iron rods and looks into the thoroughfare, and are painted red or black with gilt Chinese characters written thereon, setting forth the name of the occupant and his trade. Over each doorway is placed a board with the name of the chop, firm, or style of the master on it in colors strongly contrasting with the colors of the boards. The fronts of the shops are embellished by strips of red paper containing flowery passages from the classics. The interior of the shops are most neatly arranged with bottles, tin cannisters, boxes, almerahs, cupboards, and other receptacles for goods; and samples of the latter are displayed in all parts of the shop to attract attention. The owner and his servants are exceedingly attentive to visitors and are as keen at driving a bargain as any people in the world. A Chinese druggist's shop is quite a picture. There are numerous drawers arranged round the walls filled with drugs of every conceivable description; besides tin cannisters, bottles, unique Chinese jars, pots, deers' horns, bones of different animals, and other things.

People are constantly dropping in with prescriptions from Chinese physicians, which are forthwith made up, and the medicines neatly rolled up in paper parcels and handed to the messengers; whilst the prescriptions are stamped with the druggist's seal or chop, and filed. The Chinese doctors are considered very clever in curing fevers, diseases of the bowels, or lungs and such like; but surgery they know nothing of. They will not attempt the amputation of a limb unless it is so crushed and broken, that it would be utterly useless to leave the injured part alone. It is simply cut off and thrown aside, and the bleeding stump covered with something to staunch the hemorrhage. The writer once pointed over to some bones and asked what they were good for; the druggist replied, that they were tiger's bones, and if crushed and boiled in water the decoction would make you brave. Several of the drawers are always kept filled with black pills of various sizes; like Morrison's and other quacks' pills, a vast number must be taken at a time to prove effectual. The Chinese are famous for their liniments, and balsams, which are considered infallible in attacks of rheumatism and other inflammatory affections. Our doctors might discover most important drugs, herbs, and wondrous medicines in the Chinese shops if they would but carefully go over their contents and test them.

It is usual in the Straits to speak of well to do Chinamen as gentlemen but as a fact very few of them would be entitled to the distinction in China; and none with the exception perhaps of the Honorable MR. WHAMPOA, a member of the Legislative Council of this Colony, and Consul for China, and MR. TAN KIM CHING the Siamese Consul who has some Chinese rank, none would be allowed to stand upright in the presence of a Mandarin. Many Chinese and *Babas* however are fully entitled by their status in the Colony and the suavity of their manners, to the English title of gentlemen.

MARRIAGE

Should the immigrant be successful in his career he naturally provides himself with a wife. His courtship and marriage are thus conducted. The preliminaries are arranged by a professional bride-seeker or matrimonial agent, who makes enquiries and after finding an unmarried girl, whose parents are anxious to dispose of her, he or she (there being both male and female match makers) see her and wait on the young man with a description of the young lady and her family; should they be approved of the go-between calls upon the girl's parents with a slip of red paper containing the name of the young man, the date of his birth, the names of his parents, the place of their abode, and other particulars. If the girl's parents approve of the young man they hand the agent a slip of red paper containing similar particulars regarding their daughter and the match maker takes the two slips of paper to an astrologer to know if the union of the two persons is likely to prove propitious.

The wise man consults the stars and reveals the result. If favourable, presents are exchanged, the man sending a gold ring or two, and other jewels and the girl returns a gold hair pin or other jewel and they are then betrothed. A fortune teller is again consulted, who fixes the day of marriage and a sum of money is agreed upon to be paid to the parents of the bride. The bridegroom seldom or never sees his betrothed until the marriage day. A leg of roast pork, some dollars, two bottles of arrack or brandy, two ducks, two fowls, a small box containing the paper filled up by the astrologer or fortune-teller, in which he mentions the propitious day, and two candles ornamented with coloured paper are placed on trays, usually red trays from Birmah, and are carried by the match maker to the girl's house. She accepts one fowl, a duck, a slice of the pork, all the money and the candles which are lighted at the birth of the first male child.

Obeisance is then made to the household deity or *Tokong* as it is called which is either an idol or picture of one of their deified countrymen or women, and the match maker is told that the bride elect will be ready to receive her betrothed on the happy day. A Chinaman may have three or four wives; but the first is always looked upon with the greatest respect and treated with deference by the other wives. The children of all the wives are treated on an equal footing. As a rule in the Straits, the Chinaman has only one wife, and if he takes other women into the house they are treated as concubines. No difference is made by the fathers between legitimate and illegitimate children. The father in most cases in making his will, leaves his wealth to be divided equally amongst them all, females excepted. In cases of intestacy the property is distributed according to English law.

After the betrothal the parents of the girl prepare her clothes, and the bridegroom his house for his wife's reception. On the wedding day prayer is offered to their respective Tokongs and the bridegroom sends as much money as he can afford on a brass tray, together with four wax candles, one pair has a bird cut out in colored paper pasted on each candle; and the other pair has a paper dragon, the bird is supposed to represent a phoenix which with the dragon are emblems of conjugal fidelity. On the tray is placed the red slips of paper containing the girl's name, the names of her parents, their ages and the birth place of each; and another slip of paper containing the same particulars regarding the bridegroom and his family.

There are besides on other trays dry fish, fruits of all kinds; a silk sarong, two cotton sarongs, two pieces of white and two pieces of black cloth, five or six pairs of men's shoes, five or six pairs of women's shoes, two fowls, two ducks, a roast pig, and a roast goat, and other things. The girl accepts two sarongs, two pairs of shoes, a piece of the pig, a fowl and duck, some fruit, the paper referring to her husband and a pair of candles. She returns the remainder accompanied by a pair of shoes, a fan, a silk tie for his trowsers, a purse, two dollars, five gold buttons, two pomegranates tied together with silk thread and two bottles of lime juice as a present from herself and she places a silver coin in each ear of the roast pig. After this the go-between conducts the bridegroom and his friends to the bride's house.

Six men dressed in mandarin attire, long silk gowns and conical hats, receive them at the door and lead the bridegroom to the family altar before which he prostrates himself. The attendant then points to a seat which he takes. A little boy dressed like the men now enters with several cups of tea which he presents to the guests, every cup is emptied at a signal, cigars are smoked and *sirih** chewed. The boy then leads the bridegroom to the bride's bed chamber and the girl comes out to receive them. This is their first meeting and should she be hideous the young man's feelings may be more easily imagined than described.

The happy pair then worship together at the family altar; the man then points to the door and the girl walks out; the man points to her sedan chair or carriage waiting outside, which the bride enters followed by two young girls, the bridesmaids. A procession is formed which conducts the bride to the bridegroom's house. On leaving the residence of the bride's parents a great number of crackers are fired off for good luck.

On reaching her future home the husband comes to the sedan or carriage, strikes it with his fan and opens the door, points to the door of his own house which the bride enters. The pair then worship at the husband's family altar, after which the bridegroom points to an upper

---

Sirih, the betel pepper.— *Crawfurd.*

room where a repast is spread. Two hard boiled eggs are placed on a plate in the centre of the table. The husband and wife seat themselves opposite each other, the latter takes a chop stick and points to one of the dishes; the former does the same, and in like manner all the food is pointed out, when the man takes one of the eggs and descends to the company, and the girl takes the other egg and follows. The husband then strips himself of his marriage suit and the ceremony is completed. Three days after they worship at their own family altar and then go to the bride's parents' house to worship at their family altar. Should the husband have parents, a chair is placed on each side of the altar for them, the bride gives a cup of tea to the husband's mother, and the husband hands a cup to the father. The newly married couple now prostrate themselves before the altar and must remain in that position till their parents take hold of their hands and raise them up. The husband's mother makes the bride a present the father does the same, and after this the whole family kowtow before the idols.

During the three first days after marriage all the friends of the newly married couple send money and presents to them. On the third day after having worshipped at the house of the wife's parents as above described, they give a feast at which all the people who have sent money are entitled to attend but those who have not sent money cannot attend unless invited in writing.

At the end of the feast the husband takes his friends to see his wife they sit, eat sirih and drink tea with her. She then takes a cup of brandy or arrack in her hand and one of the visitors puts the following questions to her: What is the arrack or brandy, as the case may be, made of? The name of her clan, her father's name, his profession, and a few more questions are asked. To these questions suitable replies are dictated by the elder females of the family. The examiner drinks his arrack. Another visitor questions her, and so on until all the visitors have put a few questions to her on various subjects. She then tastes her cup and every man is in duty bound to empty his. Tea is now handed round and the bride is examined as to her domestic acquirements, after smoking and eating sirih the company retire giving the bride presents of gold ornaments, or any other gift.

On the expiration of twelve days the girl's parents give a feast to which the newly married couple are invited. After regaling themselves the bride returns to her house, before the servants or others in the house light fires, for if smoke should appear from the roof of the house before she returns it is considered an unlucky omen. On leaving her father's house two sugar canes are put on the roof of her carriage. At the end of a month the bride pays her parents a visit which ends all the ceremonies. The marriage ceremony is lengthened or shortened according to the means of the parties concerned, and the value and extent of the presents vary according to circumstances. The gist of the whole affair appears to be the interchange of the slips of red paper. These are always treasured up like our certificates of marriage and produced when proof is required of the event. In Singapore these slips of paper are taken by Hokiens to TAN BENG SWEE or TAN KIM CHING who registers the marriage and puts his seal on the papers.

As a rule the Chinese women are faithful; and the men devoted to their children. It is a pleasant sight to see after the day's work is over the men nursing their babies, or amusing their children, looking happy and contented. Parents expect much from the children, especially from the males, the greatest attention in life, and when dead the performance of the customary rites and ceremonies at their tombs. It is the belief of the Chinese that the peace of his soul depends upon the rites performed at his grave and vast sums of money are left by them with instructions in their wills for the due celebration of these posthumous rites and ceremonies called "*Sin Chew;*" and the *Baba* views with horror these pious bequests set ruthlessly aside by English judges as being superstitious and opposed to our rules against perpetuities.

The following description of *Sin Chew* as practised by the Chinese of the Straits Settlements is taken from the judgment of Sir Benson Maxwell in the suit of Choa Cheow Neoh *vs.* Spottiswoode:—

"The word *Sin Chew* is composed of *Sin,* which means a spirit, soul or ghost, and *Chew,* which means ruler; and the composite word means the spirit ruler, or spiritual head of the house. When a man dies, his name, with the dates of his birth and death, is engraved on a tablet; this is enclosed in an outer casing, on which a new name, which now for the first time given to him, and the names of his children, are engraved. This tablet is kept either in the house of the worshipper, or in that which has been set apart for the *Sin Chew.* It is sacred, and can be touched only by the male descendants or nearest male relatives of the deceased, who alone may look upon the name on the enclosed tablet. It is the representation of the deceased. At certain periods, viz: on the anniversary of his peath, and once in each of the four seasons, his son or sons, or if he has none, his nearest male relative, but never his daughters or other females, go to the place where the tablet is, and lay on a table in front of it a quantity of food, such as pigs, goats, ducks, fowls, fish, sweetmeats, fruit, tea and arrack. They light joss-sticks, fire crackers, burn small squares of thin brown paper in the centre of each of which is about a square inch of gold or silver tinsel, they bow their heads three times, kneel, touch the ground with their foreheads, and call on the *Sin Chew* by his new name to appear and partake of the food provided for him. The food remains on the table for one or two or even three hours, during which time the spirit feeds on its etherial savour; and to ascertain whether it is satiated or satisfied, two *pitis* (Chinese coins) or two pieces of bamboo thrown on the table or on the ground in front of it, and if they both turn up with the same face, the offering is considered insufficient time to allow the spirit to partake of it, the same test is again resorted to, and so, until the coins or bamboos, by turning up different faces, shew that the spirit has had enough. The food is then removed, and eaten or otherwise disposed of by the relatives, but there is no distribution of it in charity or among the poor. Indeed, the Chinese have a repugnance to food which has been offered in this way, except when they are members of the family. The papers which are burnt supply the spirit with money and clothing, the gold and silver tinsel turning into precious metal. No prayers are offered to the spirit; the person who makes the offering of food asks for nothing whatever. The primary object of the ceremony is to show respect and reverence to the deceased, to preserve his memory in this world, and to supply his wants in the other. Its performance is agreeable to God, the supreme all-seeing, all-knowing, and invisible being, who assists and prospers those who are regular in this duty; and its neglect entails disgrace on him whose duty it is to perform it, and poverty and starvation on the neglected spirit, which then leaves its abode (either the grave or the house where the tablet rests) and wanders about, an outcast, begging of the more fortunate spirits and haunting and tormenting his negligent descendant, and mankind generally. To avert the latter evil, the wealthier Chinese make, in the seventh month, every year, a general public offering, or sacrifice, called *Kee-too* or *Poh-toh*, for the benefit of all poor spirits." The real Chinaman as well as a few *Babas* remit money annually to China for the performance of the *Sin Chew* at the graves of their ancestors.

Religion does not appear to enter into the marriage rites; they appear to consist of nothing more than a series of feasts, and meaningless observances; no express contract is entered into, but the fact of its being an ancient form is sufficiently binding on the Chinaman's conscience and few instances occur of the men forsaking their wives, though their notions of morality are exceedingly lax. No restraint is placed upon the husband though the wife is expected to be as virtuous as any under the severest codes.

The following causes of divorce are enumerated in the Chinese ceremonial code: "A wife may be divorced for barrenness: for adultery; for refusing to serve her father-in-law and mother-in-law, for much speaking, for theft, for jealousy; for disease, viz: some inveterate kind of leprosy, &c." There are however three exceptions in favor of the wife, admitting even that several of the above can be clearly proved. These are, 1. "If she have mourned three years for her father-in-law or mother-in-law. 2. If when the parties are married the husband was poor, but has since become rich. 3. If at the time of their marriage the woman's parents or relatives were alive, but have since died so that she has no home left her; if any one of these things can be proved she cannot be legally put away. In case of a wife deserting her husband, the law enjoins that she be beaten one hundred blows with a rod, and leaves it at the husband's option either to give her away to another man, or to sell her. If a wife elope from her husband, and marry another man, she is to be put to death by strangling." From these notes the reader will perceive that the Chinese law is sufficiently severe in regard to the offending female. The law gives the wife no power to divorce the husband. A separation however she may claim. In the Chinese penal code there are some express safeguards for the rights of a wife, and it is provided that any man degrading his legal wife to the situation of a handmaid shall be punished with one hundred blows; and he that during the life of his legitimate spouse treats any handmaid on an equality with her shall receive ninety blows and both parties be restored to their proper stations." It is added, "He who having a wife marries another wife, shall be punished with ninety blows, and the second marriage shall be void." The notes on this law observes that "a wife is one whose person is equal in rank to that of her husband; a handmaid, one who is merely admitted to his presence." A vast deal of money is wasted in wealthy families when their children marry; and Europeans are often invited to witness a portion of the ceremony—when bride and bridegroom sit together at the conclusion to receive visitors. It is a most ludicrous sight to see the two sitting like a couple of dummies prevented from speaking or moving. The man attired in mandarin costume, the woman bedecked with jewellery of every description, wearing a high head dress glittering with jewels, and wearing a rich silk or satin suit.

CHILDBIRTH

On the birth of a child the date of birth is written on a slip of red paper which is carefully preserved. At the birth of the first male child the two candles first sent by the husband are lighted and one month after the birth the friends of the father meet together, drink arrack and chew sirih; and amongst the *Babas* the following ceremony is observed. An empty green coconut is placed in a brass pan full of water, the child's head is shaved clean and the hair is placed inside the coconut and the latter is carried to the seaside and the hair thrown into the sea. The shaving takes place in the presence of the female relatives of the child; during the operation presents for the child of bangles, brooches, or anklets are placed by the relations on the edge of the brass plate, and are taken and placed on the child.

At this ceremony the name of the child is sometimes given. A Chinese has invariably two or more names, sometimes as many as four. He has one in childhood, another at school, a third when he enters into life, and a fourth or business name which he assumes, with a chop or seal, when he opens a shop, or enters upon any other commercial undertaking by which he is known to the general public. He has also a new name given to him after death as mentioned in the description of the *Sin Chew*. It is a common practice to give the same second name to all the male children of a family, thus Chiang Hong Lim, Chiang Hong Choon, Chiang Hong Guan, Chiang Hong Lian; Tan Beng Swee, Tan Beng Gam, Tan Beng Gwat; Lim Chong Guan, Lim Chong Wat and so on. Contrary to our custom the surname comes first. There are no religious ceremonies attending the birth of a child. Male children are prized far above females; in China girls are often disposed of summarily by being left to perish in the fields or thrown into the rivers.

In the Straits infanticide is unknown and all the children male or female are well taken care of. Males are more highly regarded because parents look to them for the observances of the posthumous rites and ceremonies which give peace to their souls.

If married people have no sons they readily adopt the superfluous male children of other people, especially members of their own family, so that they may not die without leaving heirs behind them to perpetuate their memories. The adopted child assumes the surname of the clan he is received into and is regarded in the same light by the adopted parents as their own flesh and blood would be. Chinese make no difference between adopted and their own children on leaving property.

BURIAL

When a Chinese dies his face is washed and the body is dressed in a suit of white clothes; the queue is unplaited and combed out; sacred paper is burnt and lighted candles placed at the foot of the corpse and a packet of paper money is placed under the head of the corpse; joss sticks are also lighted and placed round the body; a coffin is then brought and the body put in with quicklime. In some families coffins are stored ready for use. Should the deceased have children, they, or if he is unmarried, the nearest relatives dress in sackcloth; undo their queues and make themselves look as miserable as possible, and literally howl round the coffin. A little before the coffin is removed to the cemetery tables are spread with eatables, and a priest attends to perform the funeral ceremony which is thus conducted. The relatives acting as chief mourners have lighted joss sticks placed in their hands and are made to kowtow and prostrate themselves before the tables, while the priest stands at one side ringing a small bell and chanting verses in a monotonous low tone. After keeping up the ringing for about half an hour, coolies lift the coffin and it is carried to the grave no matter how far.

This is no easy task, as the coffins are very heavy and it generally takes thirty to forty men to lift them. They divide the weight by multiplying the shoulder sticks applied to the poles. Fortune tellers, or astrologers are consulted as to a propitious day for the funeral which may be fixed by him on some day a long way off, and the body has to be kept in the house until the lucky day arrives. The astrologer is also consulted as to the best site for the grave. He does so with a compass, and does not profess to be guided by the stars or any occult science in coming to a conclusion. The writer recollects seeing a party of British seamen at the capture of Woosung in 1842 enter a Chinaman's house where were two or three coffins covered over with rich cloths highly decorated. Jack concluded they were treasure trove and commenced a violent attack upon them with axes and hatchets; and had cut into them deeply when an officer who had been in China before came in and informed them, much to their disgust, that the cases were likely to contain dead bodies and not dollars.

When the auspicious day arrives the coffin is conducted to the grave with great pomp and ceremony. The funeral procession is formed first by the chief mourners, members of the family male and female dressed in sack-cloth; followed by members of every secret or friendly society the deceased may have belonged to, marching two and two accompanied by bands of Chinese music creating the most discordant sounds. Nothing would embitter the dying moments of a Chinaman more then the fact that he would be buried without a procession and display. One motive for belonging to the secret and other societies is to insure a large attendance of persons at funerals of members; many societies exist with no other object than to afford members an ostentatious burial. The chief mourners keep up an appropriate howling as the procession moves on to show their grief for the loss of the departed. The members of the different secret societies are dressed in various uniforms so as to distinguish them. Many wear large spectacles of different colors, symbolical of something mysterious no doubt. The procession is accompanied by coolies bearing flags, umbrellas, staves with various symbols upon them, little boys on ponies disguised as old men with spectacles on; and a mixed crowd brings up the rear on foot and in carriages. The funerals of women are quite as gorgeous as those of men. The procession that accompanied the remains of the wife of the Toah Koh or elder brother of the Ghi Gock Triad Society in the early part of 1877 was fully three quarters of a mile long.

As the procession moves along gold and silver paper money is strewn about the road by two or three men who run ahead of the coffin, and at the grave a piece of white cloth about half a yard wide and a little more than a fathom long is given to each person. It is amusing to see coolies who have attended the funerals of rich people returning from the grave chatting and laughing and showing the cloth they have received to each other. When the procession arrives at a turning in the road it is usual for the chief mourners to prostrate themselves before the coffin to show respect they say to the bearers. A vast deal of money is spent on funerals.

The poor are buried with very little pomp in cemeteries which are invariably picturesquely situated on the sides of beautiful hills. And the only part of the ceremony that is never neglected even by the poorest, is the strewing of the road with paper money which the deceased is supposed to require on his passage from this world to the next. A bundle of paper money is also nailed on the coffin. The rich bury their dead in their own plantations in all parts of the country and the graves are shaped like the last letter of the Greek alphabet Omega. Emblematical of the end of all things perhaps and significant in connection with the expression in the Bible of the Alpha and Omega of all things, the beginning and ending. The graves are prettily painted and adorned and add much to the natural beauty of the scenery; some graves are of gigantic proportions and are always kept in thorough repair. In the front of each grave is placed a tablet of granite containing the name, age, and place of birth of the deceased. Twice a year the whole family repair to the grave to perform the rites and ceremonies so sacred to the Chinaman.

Amongst the rich Tay Chews, it is customary to send back the bodies of their relations and friends for internment in China and some Hokiens have done so. The freight for such cargo is very great and quite prevents people of ordinary wealth to indulge in the luxury.

The writer knows of no act that has so great an influence upon a Chinaman than the worship of his deceased ancestors. There is something selfish too in the performance thereof. He does it not so much for the benefit of the dead as for his own well being. He believes that the due celebration of these posthumous ceremonies confers luck upon himself in this life, and discontinuance or slovenly performance of them is sure to be visited by misfortune and curses of the departed. In life the Chinaman always selects the lowest spots of the earth to build his hut on as near as he can get to a spring of water. For death he selects the highest and most beautiful sites where his bones may rest in peace surrounded by the beauties of nature. With us in the Straits the reverse is the rule. We select the most beautiful spots for the living, whilst we are satisfied with low swampy sites for the resting place of our dead.

Besides the tablet placed on the tomb a small wooden tablet containing the name of the deceased with other particulars is placed in one of the rooms of the family mansion, in front of the household Gods and worshipped. At the grave the worship, or religious ceremony performed by a priest is repeated and the coffin is buried, after which a substantial repast is partaken of; the procession then is reformed and returns somewhat in the undignified style of our own funerals. At the house of mourning two lanterns of bamboo covered with white cloth on which Chinese characters are written, are hung at the door for an uncertain period from seven days to a month, after which they and other paper ornaments used for the funeral are burnt; a week after the funeral the family of deceased visits the grave again, in one hundred days, and subsequently twice a year to worship and sacrifice to the names of the departed as well as ancestors in general. If there are Budhists in the Straits they have abandoned cremation entirely. The male relations of deceased, if Hokiens, are not allowed to wear colored clothing for twelve months at least, but must always dress in white. The women mourn in black. After one hundred days those that can afford the expense have the image of the deceased and a small house fully furnished, made with bamboo paper and tinsel, burnt at the door. Cantonese do not observe this last ceremony but merely worship at the grave as above described.

The rules for mourning are as follows. A man must wear white sackcloth or other coarse stuff for a week or so for his father or mother; or grand parents. And white clothing and white thread in his queue for two years or longer; three years is the proper period; a razor must not pass over his head for one hundred days. The white thread in tail may be discarded in eighteen months. Women mourn for parents and grandparents in white for one month and in black for two or three years. With black clothing white shoes must always be worn, and silver hair pins and other jewels; whilst in mourning they may not wear gold ornaments. For an elder brother or sister males wear black clothing and blue thread in their queues. For husband or wife the same mourning as for an elder brother or sister is worn. No mourning is worn by parents for their children, nor is it necessary to wear any mourning for younger brothers and sisters. Christian Chinese adhere to the same customs with regard to mourning.

Several years ago the Roman Catholic Missionaries were exceedingly successful in converting the Chinese, especially the Kehs to Christianity. A great many chapels were built in the country districts of all the settlements and the *Hong Kahs* as Chinese Christians are called, became a powerful body. Just as in joining a secret society the converts regarded themselves as a community of brothers, and were as ready to fight as the worst of the heathen around them. They were concerned in riots that gave the authorities a great deal of trouble and which were suppressed with some difficulty. Of late years however whether the zeal of the missionary has waxed colder, or the Chinese have discovered that they acquire no peculiar privileges by becoming Christians the gospel has not spread amongst them with the rapidity of former days; many converts have recanted and returned to their former idolatry and heathenism.

In the country districts near the chapels nearly all the Chinese are still Christians, and it is a cheerful sight on a Sunday to see them, men women and children dressed in gay attire, the women with lace veils over their heads in the Spanish style, wending their way from their plantations and the adjacent villages to the chapels to attend divine worship.

One Sunday the writer visited the Bukit Timah Chapel at Singapore, the Priest was absent but on the people assembling one of them, possibly a *sinseh* or teacher, read portions of the holy Scriptures to them in Chinese, led them to chant a hymn or psalm, and lastly dismissed them with a blessing closing with the doxology. The demeanor of the whole assembly during the service was devout in the extreme, and the writer could not help being grateful for the result of the teaching of those zealous and devoted men, the Catholic missionaries, who sacrifice all the comforts of a civilized life, and undergo hardships and privations of no ordinary nature to carry the knowledge of salvation to the uttermost parts of the earth.

The adoption of Christianity must prove beneficial to the Chinese; education, morality, intelligence, and physical comforts follow in its train says Mr. CRAWFURD who states that, the Christians in the Island of Amboyna for instance are the most moral, best educated. and best conducted people of the whole Archipelago. The Protestant Missionaries have not been so successful in the Straits, but they also have their chapels here and there surrounded by a few earnest Chinese christians who are working zealously in the good cause. The writer has visited some of these chapels from time to time and has always been struck by the earnestness that prevailed amongst all attending the services. There are also Chinese girls schools in charge of earnest lady missionaries, but there are no statistics published of the result of these institutions.

WORSHIPPING THE DEAD

Every family goes to the graves of its ancestors twice a year. Eatables of various kinds are placed at the foot of each grave with chop-sticks, and joss-sticks are lighted and stuck into the ground round the grave. Each visitor takes a few in both hands and kow-tows to the ground twice, and sacred paper representing money is burnt; for the spirits of the dead are supposed to require money to buy clothes and food in the other world. After burning the paper the kowtowing is repeated and while doing so each person says "on such a day we your descendants or relations come to worship you; protect and guard us" or words to the same effect. In the meantime the ghosts of the departed are supposed to enjoy themselves over the eatables. When they are satisfied, their children return home and demolish the food left by the spirits.

The prospect of death has no fears for the Chinese, and they commit suicide on the slightest provocation. A wife will do it to revenge herself on her husband when she goes to the other world, believing that she will have the power to return at any time to vex and tease her refractory spouse. A cooly afflicted with a troublesome sore that lasts longer than he thinks necessary will coolly go out during the night and hang himself on the first tree he comes athwart. Or a trivial dispute with his master will lead a cooly to take his own life to rid himself of the annoyance. For imaginary or temporary evils they commit suicide hastily, but often will endure for years the greatest sufferings with patience and fortitude. The worship of the dead and the attention paid to their wants in the other world by the living must in a great measure conduce to this callousness of death. They have no definite ideas of what their future state may be, but are convinced, unless very wicked in this life, that they are sure to be happier in the other world than in this. The Christian's ideas are somewhat opposed to this view. However good he may be, the terrors of death and the cruel punishments awaiting him on the other side of the grave, inculcated by a false teaching, render him fearful of the change.

The Chinese are cowards only when facing their fellow creatures. The writer was informed by officers who were at the bombardment of Canton in 1860 that, when the city was in flames the inhabitants were using fire engines to put the fire out under a heavy fire of shot and shell as unconcernedly as if they were in no danger; and as they were shot down others would appear on the house tops holding the hoses and directing the supply of water to where the flames raged fiercest to be shot down in their turn. But in the field it was absurd to see hundreds of Chinese fly before half a dozen Englishmen. The writer saw in 1842 five resolute fellows armed with old Brown Bess hold in check a vast crowd armed with matchlocks and other weapons, who had not the courage to advance closer than a hundred yards. In street fights such a sight as a stand up fight between equal numbers is never seen. Invariably a crowd of armed men make a rush at a few unfortunate passers by and beat them to death, or leave them on the ground seriously injured; or swoop down unexpectedly upon a plantation, and murder every man, woman, and child there.

DOMESTIC HABITS

The domestic habits of the Chinese resemble our own to some extent. In the lower and middling classes the females of the family cook the meals and attend to the comforts of the men, and perform the menial duties of the household. The rich employ servants to execute those duties. At daylight the servant, should there be one in the house, if not, a member of the family lights a few incense sticks, comes to the front of the house and bows to the sky three or four times, holding the lighted sticks above the head. This obeisance is in honor of God they say. This is the only worship they render the Great Creator during the day. The servant then kowtows to the household gods and places the lighted sticks in stands that are placed before them for the purpose. A few of these lighted joss sticks are stuck into niches at the outer door of the house. The household gods are represented by idols or *tokongs*, or *topehkongs* as they are called by the Malays or pictures of deified personages. After the morning worship the house is thrown open and swept clean; the men go to their daily avocations and the women prepare breakfast. In the towns they breakfast between seven and eight o'clock; lunch at eleven and dine between three and four p.m. On a plantation the coolies breakfast at six in the morning and go to work after, lunch at eleven or twelve o'clock, and dine after the labors of the day are over, about sunset or a little later. The coolies are assembled by the sound of a cow's horn which is also used to collect neighbors together in cases of emergency, such as an attack of robbers or other untoward circumstance.

Men take their meals alone; women and children take theirs in an

[36]

inner apartment; there is no social intercourse between the sexes. Women are treated by the Chinese like all Eastern nations as inferior to the lords of the creation.

There is not much variety in the meals; the breakfast is as substantial as the dinner. Their staple food is boiled rice to which they add stews of different kinds made of pork, fowls, ducks, and fish cut up in small pieces and seasoned with salt, onions, and condiments of different kinds. The food has always to be cut in small pieces as the use of chop-sticks is universal. Very few, even of the wealthiest, indulge at table in European knives, forks and spoons. It requires a vast deal of practice to handle chopsticks; a pair is held between the fingers of the right hand and the food is deftly picked up with the tips and put into the mouth. When rice has to be eaten the bowl containing it is held to the mouth and the grains are shovelled in with the sticks. For the soups they use an earthen spoon shaped like a baby's papboat. As a rule the Chinese eat very fast. The flesh of the pig is more commonly used than that of any other animal.

The number of dishes that a Chinese will put on the table for European guests is something marvellous. Fish maws, bird's nests, trepan and other choice articles form the chief ingredients of the best dishes, and some are palatable enough.

At a thorough Chinese dinner ever and anon the host stops eating and challenges his guests to drink and holds up a diminutive cup filled with arrack or brandy to the brim, each guest does the same and follows the movements of his host. Each cup is emptied at the same time, and placed on the table empty. After the dinner it is considered polite to belch as loudly as possible to evince one's satisfaction. At a dinner the writer was once at with twenty or thirty *Babas* he was astonished at the individual next to him indulging not only in loud sounds from his mouth but by explosions of a different nature. The writer looked at him with disgust much to his amusement; and he excused himself by saying that unless the guests showed their approval of the repast in this way the host would fear that he had not given them a good dinner, and that they had not eaten to repletion. The superiority of the father is carried to such an absurd length in Malacca that sons cannot sit at the same table with their fathers if there are any guests present. They may attend as domestics but dare not sit at the table on an equal footing with the father.

Babas are exceedingly fond of a condiment prepared from the shrimp called *Balachan*. The shrimps are shelled and steeped in *congee,* or water that rice has been boiled in, until fermentation begins; they are then taken out of the water and dried in the sun, and finally ground to a pulp with spices, and may then be cooked in various ways; fried simply, or burnt wrapped in a piece of plantain leaf, or mixed with chillies, onions, garlic and aromatic herbs of different kinds, with various articles of food such as, prawns, fish, &c., &c., when it is called *sambal,* and it is then eaten with rice and curry or with rice alone. It is exceedingly palatable with bread and butter. *Balachan* is equal or superior to some tastes to any European caviare, or potted meats, or fish prepared with spices, but the taste for it must be acquired. The smell is decidedly objectionable.

When in England some years ago the writer had received a pot of *Balachan* from the Straits and occasionally indulged in it. The smell at a distance whilst it was being cooked was savory enough, and attracted the attention of a neighbour, a fine old English Gentleman of the old school. He asked what it was that smelt so delicious; and on a description of the stuff being give him, he said he was curious to taste it. He was invited to dinner and a delicious *sambal* was placed at his elbow to be eaten with his curry and rice. The latter he took to amazingly and he did not object much to the taste of the *sambal,* but the smell proved too much for him; he sniffed and coughed awhile and at last, unable to stand the aroma any longer, but being too polite to complain aloud, said in a stage whisper to the servant, "take this horrible stuff away and place it somewhere else". We enjoyed a hearty laugh at the old gentleman's expense. He often after enjoyed his curry and rice with us but never again was tempted to try the *balachan.* A Malacca belle prides herself on the splendid *balachan* and delicious sambals she can make. The *balachan* is decidely a delicious compound, but like the durian, the most delicious fruit in the world, is exceedingly objectionable on account of its offensive odour.

In all houses tea is infused and kept ready for use all day, for a Chinese seldom drinks plain water. They bathe frequently and at all hours of day or night. It is said if sinkeks neglect the bath they get ulcerated legs which sometimes prove incurable.

In their leisure hours the women amuse themselves by making purses, ornaments for bed hangings, children's caps, and other fancy articles. Their fancy work is exceedingly pretty and some of the commonest looking women display great ingenuity, skill and originality in the patterns they invent. Women are exceedingly fond of picnics. Every Sunday large parties of them may be seen driving out with their children to spend the day in the country feasting, bathing, and not unfrequently gambling. Sometimes they play for love as we call it, but more often for money. The love of gambling is inherent in the Chinese. Men, women and children are addicted to the vice. A species of gaming called "Wha Whay" is a special favorite with the women and a great deal of money is lost and won at this pastime. The men amuse themselves with cards, dominoes, chess, and draughts. These are somewhat similar to the game played by us. At chess no figures are used, but draughts-men are employed with Chinese characters cut into them, representing the different pieces such as pawns, kings, castles and others.

Women do not join the men in their amusements. They play by themselves, and at cards only. The Chinese games at cards are exceedingly simple, all depend upon chance. The highest card winning every thing. No skill or ingenuity is requisite to play any of their games. Young men are fond of flying kite made in the shape of birds, ships, animals, men, women, snakes and other creatures. A bow is usually attached to each kite, the strings of which vibrate in the passage of the kite through the air and produce a curious sound. Where a great number of kites are afloat their appearance is very enlivening, and the bows being of different sizes the aerial music produced is not unpleasant to the ear.

Some perform on rude guitars with one, two, or three strings, which they accompany with their voices in a shrill falsetto, most disagreeable to a musical ear. The writer has heard many players but never could distinguish any melody. There is simply a sliding up and down the strings with the finger at random whilst the strings are struck with a piece of iron producing the most extraordinary sounds. A man will amuse himself in this way for hours. They may possess tunes but the writer has never been able to detect one. A player will harp upon one string for hours and hours playing the same notes over and over again. A small fife is sometimes heard but it is not a favorite instrument. The *Babas* have got the violin from their Portuguese neighbours and can play a number of fandangoes, and European polkas, waltzes, and quadrilles. They have very good ears for music and will, if thrown with European performers catch their tunes very correctly. The Malacca *Babas* are exceedingly musical and are very clever in extemporizing words to their tunes, and will for several hours at a time amuse themselves and their guests by singing their *pantuns*, and *lagus*, accompanied by fiddles and tomtoms. The *lagus* are chiefly Malay tunes. They have an instrument which emits a tone resembling the bagpipe, which is a favorite.

It is said, as a joke, that nothing charmed the Chinese in Larut more, when Mr. Pickering the present Protector of Emigrants, who plays on the Scotch bagpipes, was sent with Major Dunlop R.A., Inspector General of Police, to Larut in Perak to settle some disputes that existed there between rival societies and tribes, causing the inhabitants of Penang a great deal of trouble and anxiety, than Mr. Pickering going about the villages playing on his pipes, Chinese tunes mayhaps. He quite won their hearts like Orpheus of old and the result was that the Chinese became most tractable.

The rival parties shook hands, peace was restored and Major Dunlop and Mr. Pickering returned to Penang with flying colors. The effect of the bagpipes was magical: When the party was marching up to a stockade and it was not quite certain how they would be received Mr. Pickering would strike up on his pipes. The Chinese would flock out of their strongholds by hundreds and regard the player with wonder, and march along in his wake seemingly delighted with what they doubtless thought was Chinese music. They have also drums, cymbals, flageolets, and wooden and metal instruments of percussion which are struck with sticks. When a host of these instruments are played at the same time, as they are at theatres and processions, the noise is as discordant as can be imagined. Noise is apparently, the desideratum.

They have no manly games. *Babas* join the Malays in their game of foot ball or "sepah ragah"; and the Klings in a game resembling "prisoner's base". They also play at pitch and toss.

Well to do *Babas* have their billiards and bowls, and other European games, but as a rule the Chinese idea of enjoyment is to sit still or lie on the back and do nothing. Nothing surprises them more than the pertinacity with which Europeans go in for exercise, walking or riding daily; playing at cricket and lawn tennis, running, jumping, putting weights, and taking other violent diversion; when it lies in his power to enjoy his *dolce far niente* without stirring, a muscle. The poor walk sturdily covering their three and a half to four miles an hour with ease; but will ride

---

Pantun a Malay word signifying a poetical sentence, consisting of four short lines rhyming alternately in which the thought is expressed by comparison or allusion. *Crawfurd.*
Lagu, tune, or air. *Crawfurd.*

in a hackney carriage whenever they can afford to pay for one. Those who can afford it keep their own carriages and pairs belonging to the rich *Babas*. The Chinese seldom ride on horseback. In Malacca the women are carried about on men's shoulders slung in a hammock screened from the sun by *Kajangs*.* The Chinese in the Straits have no particular arms or weapons. The one in common use is a sharp pointed pole sometimes tipped with iron about eight feet long resembling the ordinary boarding-pike. It is used very skilfully both for offence and defence and has the advantage of keeping the enemy at a respectable distance. It is the usual weapon used in street fights. Another dangerous weapon is the trident. This is sometimes used in riots but is not in common use. The double sword is another weapon that is used skilfully. The two swords are carried in one sheath and whilst one is used for attack the other is held in the left hand and serves as a defensive weapon. Firearms are seldom resorted to. As a rule these people are of peaceful inclination, and do not keep weapons in their houses. Even in isolated places in the country hundreds of houses may be found without a weapon of any kind. In cases of emergency the carrying pole which nearly every labourer possesses, proves a lethal weapon in the hands of a powerful man.

As a rule in the Straits the Chinese salute each other in the European fashion by shaking hands; though on ceremonious occasions they join their closed hands and lift them two or three times towards the head in orthodox Chinese fashion.

They are very polite to visitors; the wildest Chinaman on a European visiting his hut will place a tray before him with teapot and small cups of tea, and attend upon him whilst in the house and conduct him on leaving with great ceremony to the door.

Dancing is never indulged in, either off or on the stage. They go to our Balls and are doubtless shocked at the way our belles whirl about in the mazes of the waltz tightly clasped round the waist by members of the opposite sex. They form a very vague idea of our morals from such scenes, but never express their sentiments.

They are subject to leprosy and other diseases, the result it is said of the immoderate use of the flesh of the pig. They seldom or never eat that of any other animal. Beef is seldom or never touched. In spite of frequent

---

*Kajang, a dressed nipah palm leaf for a thatched roof, or awning. *Crawfurd*

ablutions cutaneous diseases are very common amongst them. Our pauper hospitals are always full of patients; the secret and friendly societies shelter many; and yet hundreds may be met in the Colony wandering about, the most disgusting sights, exciting the sympathy of passes by who invariably give them a copper or two as they shudder past.

They are exceedingly fond of country houses surrounded by gardens laid out in true Chinese fashion with fish ponds, grotesquely shaped bushes, and dwarfed plants of every variety in pots of many shapes and colors. Mr. Whampoa's garden at Singapore is one of the lions of the place, and is worthy a visit. He has in it a perfect menagerie and aviary. His orang-utan, Mahomet, is a curiosity. His manlike propensities have, it is said, quite won over some of his visitors to the Darwinian theory. Since the above was written the orang-utan went the way of all flesh, and now ornaments the Singapore Museum. The holidays of the merchants and others are invariably spent at these retreats; often innocently, but sometimes in gambling.

Some of the rich *Babas* are munificent in their gifts to public charities and institutions; the Singapore Water Works were started with a present from the late Tan Kim Seng of $13,000 to Government for that purpose and took, it deserves recording, twenty two years to finish. Mr. Cheang Hong Lim, one of the Singapore Opium Farmers, has spent large sums of money for the public benefit and gives a cup to be run for at the races, and so with the *Babas* at the other settlements.

Sometimes they spend large sums of money rather ridiculously. One gentleman it is said has a great regard for turtles, and spends a fortune in buying all he can at the different markets, and after painting his name on them letting them go at sea to revel in their native element. The name on the back the *Baba* thinks establishes his ownership and prevents the poor creatures being slaughtered if retaken. It is possible the *Baba* has some idea that the souls of his ancestors inhabit the bodies of these creatures.

The Chinese are of middling height and robust; hair invariably black, lank, coarse and plentiful on the head but deficient on face and body; they never have whiskers; if a man is fortunate enough to have a wart on the face on which a few hairs sprout, the latter are cherished with great care and allowed to grow to a great length and are much prized; but as a rule hairs of the face are carefully plucked out with pincers by the barbers.

It is a rule in China that the moustaches may not be worn till a man is a grandfather, or the beard before he is sixty years of age; but in the Straits men over forty years of age wear both, if they can get them, although childless. They may be emphatically termed a beardless race. Females are shorter than those of the European races. Pretty when young but soon become ugly and repulsive. The eyes are always black, narrow and obliquely set in the head sometimes in an angle of thirty degrees; in some faces the eye appears like a narrow slit, the upper eyelids being so tied down that the possessor has a difficulty to open the eyes, and has to throw the head back to see clearly. They have high cheek bones extending laterally, and receding foreheads; the facial angel being much smaller than in Europeans, sometimes scarcely fifty degrees; nose prominent with wide nostrils; lips thick; mouths of ordinary size; hands and feet small and well shaped; teachers, clerks, and persons of sedentary habits let the nails, of the left hand especially, grow to an inordinate length. It is a mark of gentility. Even laborers will sometimes let the nail of the left hand little finger grow long to denote his affinity to the higher classes; complexions yellowish brown sometimes very light, and when not tanned by the sun as fair as some Europeans. Teeth regular and strong, except in *Babas*, a European dentist informed the writer that they as a rule have bad teeth; *Babas* are not so robust as the real Chinese but resemble them in every other particular.

CHARACTERISTICS

The Chinese are sober, industrious, domesticated, methodical, ingenious, honest and persevering in business, respectful to their seniors, and dutiful to their parents, polite in their intercourse with each other, law loving, easily governed with firmness; on the other hand they are crafty, proud, conceited, treacherous, unscrupulous, revengeful, cowardly, cruel and untruthful. Superstitious to a degree. Their features are stolid and never indicate the working of their minds. The Chinese Sir John Davis says resemble ants, by the manner in which they conquer difficulties by dint of mere numbers; and they resemble those minute animals no less in their persevering and unconquerable industry. Many Chinese customs are just the reverse of ours. We mourn in black, they in white; we propel a boat with our backs to the bow, they with their faces to the front; we make the north point of the compass the chief point; they the south point; we take off our hats and shoes as a token

[43]

of respect, they keep them on for the same purpose; we fan our faces to cool ourselves, they fan the antipodes to produce the same effect; in our names the surname is placed last, in theirs they place the surname first; their place of honor at table is on the left side, ours is on the right; they mount their horses on the right side, we on the left; their books are written from right to left, ours from left to right; in speaking of dates they mention the year first, then the month and lastly the day of the month; we give the date first then the month and lastly the year; their women wear no petticoats and men no shirts. Mr. Wingrove Cook thus amusingly writes with reference to China and the every day customs of the Chinese. "Where the roses have no fragrance, and the women no petticoats; where the labourer has no sabbath, and the magistrate no sense of honor; where the needle points to the South, and the sign of being puzzled is to scratch the antipodes of the head; where the place of honor is on the left hand, and the seat of intellect is in the stomach; when to take off your hat is an insolent gesture, and to wear white garments is to put yourself into mourning.

FESTIVALS

No people in the world keep fewer holidays than the Chinese, they have no day of rest, no sabbath set apart to rest from labour. Their shops are open daily throughout the year with the exception of new year's day, though at that season very little business is done for several days. The new year rejoicings commence on the 30th day of the 12th moon of the old year, and conclude on the 16th day of the 1st moon. The principal days are the 30th of the old year or new year's eve, and from the first to the fifth day of the new year inclusive, and the 15th and 16th of the first moon, on which days public worship is conducted at the temples by the priests. On New Year's eve every man, woman, and child keep awake to celebrate the advent of the new year, which is ushered in by a discharge of millions of crackers. The sound is deafening and Europeans have little rest during this season. To prevent accidents the discharge of crackers is regulated by the police and restricted to certain hours of the day, when Europeans are not in the habit of going abroad. Nothing amuses young Chinamen more than throwing lighted crackers under our horses' noses and setting them off helter skelter down the streets. From midnight of New Year's eve houses are prepared for the reception of visitors who pour in to pay the inmates the compliments of the season. Visits are exchanged throughout the day and presents of tea, fruits, sweet-meats and ornaments are interchanged accompanied by letters of congratulation. Europeans make it a point to visit their Chinese acquaintances and are always hospitably received, and presented with cups of tea and other refreshments. The master of the house has to stay at home to receive visitors whilst the junior members of the family and the females pay the visits.

This task must be exceedingly wearisome to a person holding a high position although gratifying to his pride; for all day long and for several days the stream of visitors keeps pouring in and out of his house. The Honorable Mr. Ho Ah Kay Whampoa M.L.C. at the last New Year holidays commencing on the 2nd of February 1878 was besieged for eight or nine days. Hundreds of people of various nationalities called upon him, and the road his mansion stands on was rendered nearly impassable from morn to eve by the numerous carriages that bore the visitors to his hospitable gates.

The writer on the last New Year's day at the house of an influential *Baba*, a genial fellow, whose sympathies are entirely with us, was much amused by the visitors, some perfect strangers to the master of the house, rushing in, decked out in mandarin attire, long silk cloaks, conical hats, long stockings, and thick soled shoes, kowtowing half a dozen times with upraised fists, first on one side of the host and then on the other, the latter returning the bows with much good humour; then depositing their cards, narrow slips of red paper with their names and addresses written thereon on a salver, and rushing out of the house to the carriage without exchanging a word with the host. When a *Baba* came he and mine host shook hands in true English style and retired to the vestibule to hob-nob together; and so on for hours and hours. Placed against the doorway leading to his conservatory were a couple of sugar cane plants freshly cut; the writer asked his host to explain the meaning of this, but the *Baba* laughed and said he knew nothing of these things, he left such trifles to the women of his family to look after. Businessmen always close their accounts at the end of each year paying their debts and getting in all that may be owing to them and commence the year with a set of new books. It is considered unlucky to commence the year with unsettled accounts.

The 9th of the 1st moon is called the Emperor of Heaven's day and on the 15th of the 1st moon occurs the well known feast of lanterns.

[45]

Early on the morning of these holy days the men flock to the temples with sacred paper, candles, and joss sticks composed of sandal wood dust; the paper is burnt in large metal vases, and the candles and incense sticks are lighted and placed before the idols. In each house food of every description is placed before the family altar for three or four days, and crackers are burnt from three or four o'clock in the morning till late at night. On the evening of the feast of lanterns thousands of every conceivable shape and size made of bamboo, silk, and paper painted of all colours with movable figures of men, birds, and beasts revolving within are suspended in the verandahs of the houses running along the side of the streets. The lights are not very bright but the general effect is picturesque.

The scene at night in the Chinese parts of the several towns in the Colony is very exciting. Men and women walk to and fro dressed in clean holiday suits. Chinese and Malay music break on the ear as merry parties pass and repass in hired carriages; groups of Chinese are crowded round the stands of fortune tellers. Children decked out in fantastic clothing are drawn about in miniature carriages by Javanese and Boyanese coolies. Here an excited group is listening attentively to a street reader, who is reciting the accounts of some wonderful incident that occurred ages ago. There, an immense crowd is amused with the antics of a lad dressed in a strange caterpillar looking disguise, with a monstrous head having a faint resemblance to a tiger's, who jumps about and howls accompanied by the most unearthly music; this is called the game of tigers. The body of the animal is sometimes twenty feet long and is supported by boys who wriggle about from side to side imitating the movements of a living creature. The figure is a great deal more like the great sea serpent's than that of a tiger. On each side of the street stalls are placed illuminated by colored lanterns, behind which master Fucki sits retailing sweets, and cooling drinks of all descriptions and attracting the attention of passengers by knocking two pieces of wood together. And from the streets merry parties may be seen inside the shops and private houses, enjoying themselves at cards, music, songs and other amusements.

On mentioning the Chinese game of tigers, the writer is reminded of the manner in which the gamin or *Jawi Pukan** of Penang, (a mixed breed between the Kling or Bengali and the Malay) personates the royal animal. During the feast of the Mohorum several of these men go about

---

Jawi Pukan, or *Jawi bukan*, The Malay of the town, or not a Malay, a half breed.

with their bodies painted like tigers, and their hands and feet concealed by cases shaped like the paws of that animal with sharp claws attached; a tail is stuck on behind, and a chain is fastened round the waist which is held by one or two men who are supposed to be their keepers. The tigers are generally muscular clean made fellows and imitate the movements of a wild beast admirably. They carry the resemblance so far and work themselves up to such a pitch of excitement that if a live kid is thrown to them, they will seize it, tear the poor creature to pieces and drink its blood; the writer never witnessed such a performance but has heard it described and has no reason to disbelieve the story. There are families in Penang that bear among the natives the soubriquet of tigers. The child is taught to personate the animal by his father as soon as he is strong enough to bear the fatigue. On going round the town and country these tigers collect a great deal of money, and are allowed to seize any articles of food that may be exposed for sale on the road side. The writer has seen a tiger in passing down a very short street, collect a great number of coconuts, sugar canes, cakes and sweetmeats.

On one occasion a tiger was displaying his agility to the wondering crowd at Datu Kramat in Penang and had abstracted several articles from various stalls with impunity and was about to take a coconut from the stall of a young Malay, evidently a raw hand from Province Wellesley, who did not, or would not, see the joke; master tiger put his paw on the nut and was about to roll it away when he was surprised by an ominous shake of the head; that and the sight of a thick stick which the Malay held under his arm ready for action, made the tiger hesitate; he essayed several times, but still the same portentous shake of the head appalled him. Not a word was said by the Malay, but there was no mistaking his eye, it seemed to say, "try it my good fellow, and you shall feel the weight of this stick." The tiger at length, not anxious to measure his strength with the sturdy chap before him, very wisely sneaked off to the next stall, where a better tempered fellow presided followed by shouts of laughter from the crowd. Some of the Jawi Bukans are however very plucky fellows. The writer saw one, a Policeman, have a stand up fight with an English sailor, a bigger man than himself, and go through several rounds in orthodox style, guarding and hitting out like a prizefighter.

During the New Year gambling is rife in all quarters. When the writer first settled in the Straits nearly thirty years ago, gaming was permitted at this festive season by the authorities and little harm ensued. In these days the laws against gaming are severe and the Police dare not permit public gaming, but doubtless there is as much of it now carried on in private as in days of yore.

The next general festival takes place in the 3rd moon when the dead are worshipped. The manner in which this ceremony is performed has been already described. On the 5th day of the 5th moon a deified magistrate is worshipped. In former years at Penang some ceremony used to take place in boats but this has long been discontinued. From the first to the 30th day of the 7th moon evil spirits, or rather the spirits of the dead are conciliated or worshipped. During this month the spirits are supposed to wander about the earth and if not propitiated plague the offenders with divers pains and aches and more serious mishaps. Long tables are spread with all the delicacies of the season and placed opposite the temples, and in other convenient places, exposed to the open air or under rough sheds erected for the occasion. Amongst the food are conspicuous the animals sacrificed to the names of the dead, chiefly pigs, goats, fowls and ducks; which are roasted whole and placed on the tables in all their hideousness. The tables are ornamented with artificial flowers, fish, and fruits, and are well worth seeing. The spirits feast during the month to their hearts' content and at the end of the ceremony, the viands are disposed of by the living. The following festivals are celebrated exclusively at the temples and are not observed by the general public. The Virgin of Lotus flower's day on the 19th of the 2nd moon. The Arch guardian of Heaven on the 3rd day of the 3rd moon. Day of the first priest on the 8th of the 4th moon. Charitable commander in chief 13th of the 3rd moon. Priest who died in celibacy 19th of the 6th moon. The 15th of the 8th moon is a festival. At Penang the three following days are celebrated at the temple where teachers, learned men, and philosophers are supposed to assist. The Inventor of letters' day, the 3rd of the 3rd moon, Confucius' birth day the 4th of the 11th moon. The above are doubtless celebrated at the three settlements of the colony as well as in Penang. The inventor of carpentery is worshipped by carpenters only, on the 13th of the 6th moon. His image is carried in procession by the fraternity from the house of the ex Loo Choo or elder, to the temple and thence to the newly elected elder's house, where it remains for twelve months. For several evenings the common people are treated with a wayang or theatre at the expense of the guild. These performances cost

[48]

as much as one hundred and twenty dollars or more a night. Other trades have their guilds and their idols and similar processions.

In Singapore on the 26th of the 10th month the Tay Chews carry their idol in procession from their cemetery at Tanglin to their temple in Philip Street to see the theatricals held there in his honor. The idol is kept there till the 11th moon when it is carried back with the same ceremony. The Hokiens have a similar procession once in three years; the idol at their cemetery on the New Harbour road is carried in procession through the parts of the Town chiefly inhabited by Hokiens to the great Hokien temple in Teluk Ayer Street, where it is left for a short period and then taken back to its own temple at the cemetery. Their procession is gorgeous in the extreme and costs the Hokien community a large sum of money. It is accompanied by coolies bearing flags, umbrellas, symbols, sedan chairs, and bands of music making the most horrible din. One wonders that such practical people, whose whole time is devoted to the acquisition of wealth should waste their money upon such absurdities; yet they can be scarcely ridiculed when we think of the absurd processions that occur in civilized London. The writer witnessed the Lord Mayor's show in 1874 and was much struck by its strong resemblance to the Chinese processions in the Straits.

Although thousands of Chinese flock to witness these processions no shops are closed; business is carried on uninterruptedly throughout the year. It is amazing to see the indefatigable perseverance and industry with which tradesmen work at their trades; goldsmiths, tailors, blacksmiths and others may be seen daily working hard from early morn to a late hour at night; and yet the health of the population does not appear to be the least affected from the want of rest and unceasing labor. This attention to work and absence of holidays may account in some measure for the sobriety of the Chinese. They have no spare time to waste in eating and drinking. It is an unusual sight to see an inebriated Chinese rolling about the streets. In the five years that the writer was a Police Magistrate he does not remember a single Chinaman being brought before him for being drunk and disorderly. On the 24th day of the 12th moon all the gods and goddesses and other celestial beings, who are on the earth ascend to heaven to report progress to their master. The festival is universally observed.

The doors of many Chinese houses, especially these of the several secret and friendly societies have the following figure described upon them, painted white and red; or black and white.

[49]

It is called Tae-Keih, Davis says, "it represents the origin of all created things, or the *premier principe material* as it is called in French translations. On the semidiameter of a given circle describe a semicircle and on the remaining semidiameter, but on the other side describe another semicircle. The whole figure represents the Tae-Keih, and the two divided, portions formed by the curved line typify what are called the "Yang" and "Yin"; in respect to which this Chinese mystery bears a singular parallel to that extraordinary fiction of Egyptian mythology, the supposed intervention of a masculo-feminine principle in the development of the mundane egg. The Tae-Keih is said to have produced the "Yang" and "Yin" the active and passive, or male and female principle and these last to have produced all things. This idea seems to have been very general; the Hindus have it and so had the Greeks." By *Babas* it is called "Jit-Goeh," Sun and Moon, and when surrounded by an octangular figure it is called "Pak Kwa."

CHINESE CHESS

The game is played upon an oblong board marked out into sixty four divisions; there are two sets of pieces of opposite colours, of sixteen men each, and of various powers. These sets of men are arranged opposite to each other, and attack, defend, and capture like hostile armies. A river is supposed to separate the two armies having thirty two squares on each side. The accompanying diagram will best explain the name and place of each man at the commencement of the game. These moves may be briefly described as follows: The soldiers or pawns advance along the line they are placed upon until they cross the river into the enemy's board, when they move like our castle in every direction along the lines a single square at a time; and capture pieces in their way in straight lines.

A cannon like our castle moves any number of squares forwards, backwards, or sideways but cannot capture a piece if another piece intervenes. This piece may cross the river. The *Elephant* like our Bishop moves diagonally, two squares at a time and is confined to the sixteen squares on his side of the board, and may not cross the river; or to the side of his fellow Elephant. The *Horse* like our Knight moves one square forward or backward, and one diagonally, but cannot capture if a piece stands on the angle when he moves diagonally. He may cross the river. The *Carriage* or *Castle* moves exactly like our castles, any number of squares backwards and forwards or sideways but not diagonally; and may cross the river.

The *Captain* or *King* and *Scholars* or *Councillors* are confined to the four squares marked with diagonal lines at the head of the board which may be called the citadel or fort. The *Captain* moves only one square at a time in any direction along the lines in his citadel. He cannot be taken; and when attacked must interpose one of his pieces or move out of check, unless the checking piece can be captured. When there is no means of rescuing the Captain the game is over.

The *scholars* move along the diagonal lines within the citadel. The pieces that may cross the river into the enemy's board are the soldiers, cannons, horses and carriages; and it must be observed that all the pieces move along the lines and always stand where the lines cross each other and are never placed on the squares as we place them at chess or draughts. The writer was taught the Chinese game some years ago and played it with the Chinese but found it uninteresting. It requires little or no skill.

CHINESE TEMPLES

In Singapore the Tay Chews have two in Philip Street within the same enclosure, dedicated to the idol "Gwan Thien Siang Tey," and several about the country called by the same name. The buildings in Town are very old and much neglected, there are no priests attached to them; and are in charge of a Kling policeman. In each building sits a Chinese ready to sell incense sticks, and sacrificial papers to worshippers. A fortune teller has a stall there also. He sits at a table with a tray before him in which are placed a number of folded papers. He also has a glass slate, indian ink, and hair pencils at hand. For a few cents he told the writer his fortune, and appeared highly amused at a European favoring him. One of the folded papers was selected and opened. On it appeared a Chinese character. This the fortune teller copied on the slate and surrounded it with a number of strokes which appeared to resemble portions of Chinese letters. He then muttered a formula and ever and anon completed the half written characters; or added a stroke here and a stroke there until his incantations were complete. By this time the letters were finished and assumed the shape of well-known Chinese characters. He then commenced repeating the result in a loud tone. Till the end of the current year 1877 the writer was to be unfortunate but after that he would be lucky and grow rich. That his lines were cast in pleasant places and he ought to be thankful. He then smiled complacently and said the oracle had finished. The writer moved on making way for a sturdy Tay Chew cooly who appeared highly satisfied with the result and seemed anxious to obtain as favorable a fortune told for himself. The Chinese have great confidence in these fortune tellers, and scarcely undertake an event in life without consulting them or the idols.

In each temple were dingy pictures and images placed in niches far back with stands and vases full of artificial flowers and burnt out incense sticks, with numerous lanterns and glass lamps hung from the rafters, or placed on the stands. Behind the temples are a few rooms filled with portions of small carriages and sedan chairs which are put together and used in processions. In each temple are stone tablets let into the wall perpetuating the names of the original subscribers. In the front of the temples is a large flagged square surrounded by a high wall, in which temporary stages are erected for theatrical performances; when of course the place is crowded by worshippers, who are attracted more by them, than the service of the gods. Chinese gods appear to be particularly fond of the drama. The wise say that these performances are often given to screen gamblers who play in adjoining houses, whilst the attention of the police is attracted to the crowd before the theatre. Chinese worship consists in lighting incense sticks and placing them before the idols; burning sacrificial paper and bowing two or three times, or kowtowing, before the images. Heart worship there is none. Except at festivals there is no worship of any kind conducted in these Tay Chew temples. In the temples in the country live one or two men who sweep them daily and make a living by selling incense sticks, sacrificial paper and candles to worshippers; besides pocketing the alms that are bestowed upon them. Some of these men get as much as thirty dollars a month; and others grow rich; these posts are coveted and strenuous efforts are made to get them. In each of the Town temples are staves placed in racks with symbols resembling the sun, moon, swords and other things placed on their tips conveying doubtless a deep signification to the learned; but certainly none to the common herd, who have never been able to afford the writer the slightest information on the subject. There is no indication of the Budhist religion in these temples. No idols or pictures of Hindu deities are in them. It is undoubted that the Chinese in the Straits do not pretend to worship any idol or picture representing God, but only those of deified human beings who are supposed to intercede with the Almighty for mortals below.

THE HOKIEN TEMPLE AT SINGAPORE

This is a handsome building about sixty feet wide and one hundred and twenty long. It is built in imitation of the temples in China. It has five doors covered with a roof; the pillars, rafters, and beams being beautifully carved in the most fantastic devices; and richly painted with gold and vermilion. The main entrance is guarded by two stone lions, one with its mouth closed; the other with it slightly open with a ball of stone inside far larger than the aperture of the mouth, which must have been sculptured inside as it is far too large to have been inserted, Over the centre door is the name of the temple "Thien Hok Keong." The temple is built on a piece of ground purchased by the Hokiens for the purpose, and the names of the original subscribers are perpetuated on tablets built into the wall of the gateway. The temple was long under the care of the late Tan Tock Seng, who was treated as the head of the Hokiens when Singapore was first settled; and since his death the building has been under the special care of his son Tan Kim Ching the Siamese Consul, who is called the *Captain China* by his countrymen although the title and position have long since been abolished by the Government. Great credit is due to this gentleman for the care he takes of the temple and the beautiful order he keeps it in. Although it is frequented by the Chinese of all sections it is called the Hokien temple.

After passing through the gateway you cross an open paved square courtyard. At the entrance of the temple is placed a large pagoda shaped urn in which sacrificial papers are burnt. The principal temple is then entered; a large building dedicated to the virgin goddess "Thien Siang Seng Bo" commonly called "Mah Choh Poh." She is the Queen of Heaven, "Tien-how;" Davis says "she is worshipped by the Budhists, concerning whom the legend says, that she was a native of Fuhkien and distinguished in early life for her devotion and celibacy. She became deified during the 13th century under the Soong dynasty and, having originated in a maritime province she is the peculiar patroness of sea-faring people, who erect altars and temples to her on shore, and implore her protection on the water. She is supposed to have control of the weather; and in seasons of severe drought the government issues proclamations, commanding a general fast and abstinence from animal food; the local magistrate in his official capacity, goes to the temples and remains fasting and praying for successive days and nights, supplicating for rain."

The main building is supported by highly carved granite pillars brought from China, and the roof is a blaze of gold and vermilion. The carving is most ingenious and appears in every nook and corner. Numerous handsome lanterns hang suspended from the rafters. On the right of the goddess is an idol called "Kwan-teh-yia" or "Heap Thien Thie Teh," he guards it is said the entrance of heaven. On the left is the idol called "Tai-to-kong" or "Po-Seng-Thie-Yeh," he watches over the sick and afflicted. Both these idols represent jolly looking elderly gentlemen, evidently ancient sages. On the right and left of "Mah Choh Poh" standing on the floor of the temple are huge figures with hideous faces, the one on the left pointing to his ear; the one on the right having large prominent eyes, and painted a dark brown color. The first represents an attendant of the virgin who hears everything, and the other an attendant who sees further than most people. Possibly the two figures are symbolical of the all seeing and all hearing attributes of the favorite goddess. These two images are common in the temples in China. Before the goddess are placed two gigantic imitations of wax candles eight or ten feet long and about five-inches in diameter painted red; also three or four great false incense sticks; the tops of these are hollow and on festivals, lamps are placed in the candles and incense sticks and lighted. To lookers on the candles and joss sticks look real and have a fine effect. On tables placed before the idol are immense brass urns and vases to hold incense sticks that are lighted and placed there by worshippers. Flower vases and ornaments of divers kinds are placed before the goddess, the gifts of devout and pious Chinamen.

Under one of the tables are the figures of two stone animals with a young one between said to represent a tiger, tigress, and their cub; but it is difficult to say what they represent unless some mythical characters worshipped by the Chinese which are represented by these grotesque figures. People who reside in country places propitiate the tigers it is said by being respectful to these figures. So a few incense sticks are placed before them and obeisance made.

Behind the main temple is a small building devoted to the worship of Buddha. His figure, the well known cross legged image of Ceylon, Birmah, and India, is enthroned on a table by himself, rather more elaborately decorated than he is usually seen. On his head is placed a Chinese skull cap, and on his shoulders a blue satin cloak. Immediately behind on a high stand are the figures of the Hindu trinity or Budhist triad and before them three other images; one unmistakably, the many armed Doorgah of the Hindu mythology. Most of these images are draped in blue satin. There are six priests attached to this temple, and the building is in charge of a Hindu policeman..

On tables set before "Mah Choh Poh" in the main building are placed the usual crescent shaped lots having a flat and convex side; these are frequently used. Lots are also placed before "Kwan-teh-yia" and Tai-to-kong." These idols are continually consulted upon every conceivable emergency. If a man is about to venture upon any enterprise he appears before the virgin, or one of the other idols, takes up the lots and throws them up in the air. If they fall with both flat sides uppermost, the venture will prove lucky, the god is supposed to be pleased. If both convex sides are up the god is displeased and the enterprise must be abandoned. If one flat and one convex side appear, then the omen is considered the luckiest and on no account to be abandoned. Before the last mentioned idol on each side supposed to be messengers who are ready to obey the behests of their masters. The goddess and the two idols are merely regarded as intercessors.

Upon the right and left of the temples are rooms separated by twenty or thirty feet from the temples. In one of the rooms on the right is an idol called "Khia Lam Yia." He inquires into the conduct of the dead on their leaving this world. Those who have done good in this world are sent back again as rich and lucky men as a reward for their good conduct; and those who have done evil are sent back as tigers, buffaloes, alligators, or beasts of burthen to suffer for their wickedness. In the Chinese Gleaner Dr. Morrisson says "After the trials are over (at death) the more eminently good ascend to paradise; the middling class return to earth in other bodies, to enjoy riches and houses; while the wicked are to remain in hell, or transformed into various animals, whose disposition and habits they imitated during their past lives."

[55]

At four o'clock in the morning and again at four in the afternoon service is conducted in the Buddhist temple. The priests are closely shaven and with one or two exceptions are intelligent looking men. They have enough to live on and are allowed a cook to provide their daily meals. As the bell strikes four one of the priests dresses himself first in a white surplice, and over that he wears a long grey coat. He then lights two lamps before Buddha, takes a short rolling pin in each hand, opens a book written in Chinese characters and commences to chant in Gregorian tones very slowly, raising and lowering his voice from time to time melodiously enough and striking at certain pauses, first with the stick in his right hand on a hollow tortoise shaped piece of wood; and then with his left hand on a clear sounding metal bell. Occasionally striking with both hands at the same time. This performance on the bell and tortoise is probably to keep the god wide awake. The chanting gets faster and faster as the priest goes on. The Chinese who had assembled in curiosity, and those who accompanied the writer were certainly unimpressed by the ceremony. One man learned in Chinese classics, who spoke Malay fluently told the writer that, he did not understand a word that the priest was saying, and he was sure the priests were as ignorant themselves. We asked a priest if he understood the books; he said no, that it was a sacred and mysterious language understood only by the gods. The Baba read a page of the book aloud, the words were Chinese it is true, but conveyed no meaning to the reader's mind nor to the minds of those who were listening. The priests said the books had been brought from China.

Gutzlaff relates in his journal of a voyage along the coast of China in 1832-33 the following particulars of a similar service performed in a Budhist temple in China. "We were present at the vespers of the priests, which they chanted in the Pali language not unlike the Latin service of the Romish church. They held their rosaries in their hands, which rested folded upon their breasts; one of them had a small bell, by the tinkling of which their service was regulated; and they occasionally beat the drum and large bell to rouse Budha's attention to their prayers. The same words were a hundred times repeated. None of the officiating persons showed any interest in the ceremony, for some were looking around, laughing and joking, while others muttered their prayers. The few people who were present, not to attend the worship, but to gaze at us, did not seem in the least degree to feel the solemnity of the service."

Davis says that the books of the Budhist religion, which are read and chanted in the Budhist temples, are partly translated into Chinese from the originals in the Pali language, a dialect of the sanskrit; Davis also gives the following passage from the Chinese Gleaner on the subject. "The sacred language of the Budhists is called the language of "Fan" which is the name of the birth-place of Budha. It is totally unknown to the Chinese generally, and the priests themselves know nothing of it, beyond the sound of a few favorite words and phrases. The priests ascribe miraculous effects to the use of the written character and of the oral language, and consider both of celestial origin. To the repetition of the bare sounds without regard to the meaning they attach the highest importance hence they go over the same words hundreds and thousands of times. And so the senseless reading of the Koran by the Mahomedans."

The *Baba* said he had visited this temple all his life; he knew the Gods were Hindu, and that the priests eat only vegetables; no flesh could they eat; and they were sworn to celibacy but what the religion meant he knew not. Nor could he tell more about the Queen of Heaven in the big temple and the other gods there. He visited the place on festivals; lit his incense sticks, burnt sacrificial paper, made his obeisance to the idol and went his way rejoicing. He fully believed in the transmigration of souls, and the return of the wicked to the earth in the shape of animals.

In the Budhist temple hang four ancient pictures, very dirty, and nearly effaced; they have hung there ever since the temple was built and may not be removed. Each picture has a legend attached to it of the most childish nature. They are called the tiger picture; the water miracle; the bird picture; and the discovery of fire. The *Baba* related the following legend in connection with the tiger picture. Hock Leong was a wicked priest and fell into bad straits when one day accompanied by another wicked priest he went to an old woman's house and begged for food, said he and his companion were dying for want of something to eat. The old lady took compassion on them and immediately commenced to chase a cock which was feeding in the yard. The priest at this moment saw a grasshopper fly into a spider's web and fall into the spider's clutches and the cock ran up and swallowed the spider and his victim. The old woman caught the cock and killed it. The priests said they could not eat the cock because he had three spirits in him; the spirits of the spider, and grasshopper besides his own. As the old woman had nothing else to give them they wandered on. After several days of fruitless search for food Hok Leong told his friend to leave him to die, which he did, and the former went to the sea-side to drown himself. He cast himself into the sea when a great sea dragon, doubtless the sea serpent, took him up and carried him off to a place of bliss. The other priest went into the forest to kill himself when he met an immense tiger. The wicked priest asked the latter if he would eat him, he said no, and did not; but helped him in some way to relieve his hunger, and then told him to get on his back, which he did, and he was also borne aloft to a place of happiness. Why the wicked priests should have been so blest deponent sayeth not. Another legend: The discoverer of fire set out to find out for himself where fire was got from; and after several days of search and much fatigue when he was about to give in he threw himself down on a rock to rest his weary limbs, and there meditated. A happy thought occurred to him and in his joy he struck his staff into the ground when to his surprise a flame of fire issued. The old gentleman had been sitting on a volcano and did not know it. However he discovered that the centre of the earth was fire and thence the phenonemon issued. This discoverer of fire was also translated to heaven or paradise. The heathens of old said that Prometheus stole fire from heaven and introduced it to man, but the Chinese legend ascribes the introduction to a different source.

The *Baba* had forgotten the legends connected with the bird picture and water miracle. In each however the hero ends by being translated to heaven and becoming a god. The temple faces the sea, and opposite the gateway, across the public road, a rich Chinese gentleman, Mr. Cheang Hong Lim, the present Opium Farmer has built a theatre and presented it to the trustees of the temple for the performances of plays during the festivals. The plays can be clearly seen by "Mah Choh Poh," and her attendant gods through the gateway. Occasional performances are given by men who are lucky in business and make extraordinary hits often the result of the lucky omens of the gods. The priests were very polite and hospitable placing before us small cups of delicious Bohea and drinking with us with great gusto; saluting and bowing with usual Chinese dignity and grace. One of them who had just arrived from China would have been better for a good scrubbing. Marriages amongst the Hokiens are sometimes celebrated in one of the side rooms of this temple; and Mr. Tan Kim Cheng has wisely established a registry of marriages amongst his countrymen on his own authority, which is becoming generally availed of by the people, and must be found exceedingly beneficial to the Chinese community.

THE CHINESE TEMPLE AT PENANG

This temple is in Pitt Street, built on a piece of land granted by the Government to the Chinese community in perpetuity for religious purposes. The older part consists of a hall forty feet square, having a paved terrace in front, on which stand two lions and an urn in which sacrificial paper is burnt. The lions are painted green, red and black. Before the entrance to the hall a substantial railing is placed to keep the mob out on great days when it is necessary for the priests alone to worship. Within the rail, on the right hand side, the names of the erectors of the temple, with the sums subscribed by each, are cut on a piece of granite which is let into the wall. The front of the building is decorated with carved work, gaudily painted. There are three doors leading into the hall; over the centre door is a black-board which bears the words "Kong Hok Keong" which indicates that the building was erected by Macao and Hokien men conjointly. Over each side door two boys are represented holding up a Chinese cash or mace (a brass coin with a square hole cut in the centre). There is nothing striking in the appearance of the entrance. The tiles and rafters are exposed to view, and the pillars supporting the roof come down very awkwardly on either side of the altar. In the centre, with its back to the wall is a wooden house containing six images, the principal is called "Kwan Yin Hwut Chia" the virgin of the lotus-flower. The second figure is "Mah Chow Poh" the patroness of virgins, the Queen of Heaven, and the remaining four figures are attendants. The house, or box, in which these idols are placed may be closed on both sides so that a devout worshipper may enter and seclude himself from the gaze of the multitude.

In the front of this house a hole about five feet square is left open from which the idols command a view of the sea. It is supposed that the gods are particularly gratified by a fine prospect, and the Chinese endeavoured to buy up the ground in front of the temple as far as the sea so as to keep it free of buildings. But some years ago the proprietor, not a Chinaman, of a plot of ground in Beach Street refused to sell his land and built a fine house thereon, intercepting the view of the sea and Province Wellesly from the temple. The Chinese console themselves by declaring the house unlucky and under the ban of the gods. About three feet from the idols' house stands an altar on which is placed an oblong metal urn to hold incense sticks. On each side of the altar there is a wooden stand with a circular top having spikes on which candles are stuck; two pieces of bambu about a foot long, containing one hundred slips of bambu bearing Chinese characters referring to the sixty drawers of a bureau standing not far off, and two pairs of bambu lots. About four feet from the altar stands a long table on which is placed a wooden vase for incense sticks. Before the table an oblong stand with spikes for candles. About a foot from the latter are two square red tables on which votive offerings are placed. To the right is suspended a large metal bell, and on the left a drum, which are sounded on some of the great feast days. From the roof are suspended lanterns of different shapes, the gifts of wealthy Chinese. In one a light had been kept burning for several years when the writer visited it in 1851. On either side of the hall stands are placed, in which are fixed staves surmounted by representations of the sunk moon, an axe, a sword, and a dragon. Near the bell is a bureau with sixty small drawers each drawer containing questions on certain subjects corresponding to the bambu slips that are placed on the altar.

Another hall also forty feet square stands in the front of the one described separated by an open paved court yard also forty feet square. This hall contains images of the arch guardian of heaven, the charitable commander in chief, and the other idols worshipped on certain days as above related. This hall contains lanterns, urns, and candle sticks, as in the front hall. On the back of the first hall one of their deified philosophers attended by seven or eight worshippers together with the symbols similar to those placed in the hall are painted. An open yard divides both halls or temples from the priests' quarters, where they have a sleeping room, kitchen, and chapel with a lumber room. The priests attached to the temple, as in Singapore, are natives of Fuhkien and are paid by voluntary subscriptions; they also receive a dollar for each funeral they attend and a dollar for each theatrical exhibition facing the building. Two Loochoos or head men are elected annually by the Chinese community who collect money for wayangs and festivals.

When any man is desirious of undertaking any enterprise, the two virgins must be consulted; and if they do not return a favorable answer the project is abandoned, whatever it might be. The goddess' opinion is thus obtained; the bambu containing the slips is shaken till one of them drops out, the lots which are pieces cut from the roots of the bambu in the shape of cachu nuts, having a flat and a convex side, are then thrown in the air and if they fall with both convex or both flat sides uppermost, the slips of bambu are shaken and the lots are thrown over and over again till one convex and one flat side appear uppermost: this is sometimes done half a dozen times before the question is asked. When the lots fall the right way the slip of bambu that is shaken out is taken to the priest who looks at the writing on the slip and opens the drawer it refers to, from which a colored paper containing the question is taken. The inquirer then takes the paper and puts it into a box which stands near the images of the virgins, the lots are again thrown up and the inquirer must be satisfied with the first answer. If the lots fall with both plain or convex sides uppermost the answer is no; if one flat and one convex side turn up the reply is favorable.

OPIUM SMOKING

The most pernicious habit indulged in by the Chinese is the immoderate use of opium, or a preparation of that drug called *chandu*. The following is the method of preparing opium for smoking. Two balls of opium are cut open and their contents put into an iron pan which is placed on a slow fire; a man keeps stirring it with a piece of wood till the whole is dissolved; it is then divided and placed in two pans, these are inverted over the fire and baked till all moisture is absorbed. The opium can then be peeled off in slices. The hide or skin which was stripped off the balls is boiled in water till all the opium is extracted from it. The water is then strained and poured over the slices of opium which are placed in pans. Baskets are now prepared by lining them with several layers of common China paper, and they are filled with the slices of opium and placed over pans. Boiling water is then very slowly poured into the baskets over the opium. The boiling water dissolves the opium and filters through the paper into the pans. When all the opium is dissolved the pans are placed over large fires and the opium water is boiled till it thickens to a proper consistency. During the boiling a man stands by with a bunch of feathers, with which he wets and moistens the pans above the surface of the liquid to keep the latter from burning; and also brushes off all dirt which may float to the top. When the preparation can be drawn out of the pan two or three feet high without breaking it has boiled sufficiently. The pans are then taken off the fire, placed on the ground and the *chandu* cooled with fans. When quite cool it is poured into boxes ready for sale. It is always adulterated by pouring dissolved sugar candy into the opium water before it is boiled. In the Opium Farm one-fourth of a catty of sugar is added to two balls of opium; the manufacturers of illicit *chandu* mix half a catty of sugar or more with two balls of opium. The farmer sells *chandu* at one dollar and fifty cents a tahil, the sixteenthpart of a catty, which is a pound and a third avoirdupois. In all opium shops a piece of cloth is kept near the retailer, on which he wipes his fingers, knives or any article soiled with *chandu;* this cloth is used till well saturated and is then sold for a few cents. This rag is steeped in water which is strained and boiled till *chandu* is obtained, into which young sugar cane leaves chopped up very fine, are thrown and well mixed, the result is rolled into pills sold and eaten. This preparation is called *muddeth.* Opium is also eaten by many. *Chandu* is a deadly poison, of which a quarter of a dollar's weight will kill a man in an hour.

The best antidote for opium poisoning is oil, generally that of the coconut; it produces instant vomiting. Should the *chandu* have been dissolved in arrack or water, the oil will not have the desired effect. In such cases a feather introduced into the gullet will cause the patient to vomit. The sulphate of copper is also a good antidote.

Chandu is thus smoked: the smoker takes a pipe, on the bowl of which a convex piece of tin is fitted, having a very small hole in the centre. The smallest quantity of *chandu,* about the fifteenth part of a tahil, is placed on the hole, the smoker lies down and applies the *chandu* to the flame of a small lamp; he imbibes the vapour and in a few seconds the *chandu* is burnt out the refuse falling into the bowl. After a pipe has been used for some time the tin lid is taken off and the refuse is scooped out of the bowl; it is called *Tye chandu* and is retailed by the opium shop keepers and in the smoking shops, at about seventy cents a tahil, and is much used by the poorer classes. The Opium Farmers at the several settlements employ a great number of people as retailers, opium testers, water carriers, and revenue officers.

Though a great deal of smuggling is carried on and large quantities of illicit *chandu* sold, the farmers of the three settlements must derive a very large profit to be able to pay to the Government the enormous sum of dollars 731,592 per annum. An inveterate smoker will consume half a tahil or more at a time; he then falls back on his couch and sleeps off the effects; it is remarkable that an opium smoker does not sleep long; on awakening each time he returns to his pipe till sleep closes his eyelids again. The immoderate use of the drug for a few years completely destroys all a man's energies and renders him entirely unfit for active employment. The opium smoker may be readily known by his emaciated woebegone appearance. On the other hand a moderate use of opium seems to injure no more than any other poison temperately used like alcohol or nicotine. The writer has never been able to ascertain from Chinese opium smokers if the results are the wonderful visions that followed the smoking of the great English opium-eater. The Chinese aver that the use of the drug allays pain and produces profound sleep. De Quincey's visions were possibly the result of a highly imaginative mind.

GAMBLING

The Chinese and all the natives of the Straits seem to have an inherent love for gambling. Men, women and children indulge in it to a frightful extent in one shape or another. To many it is a matter of business; they form a company and start a gaming house, participating in the gains but never appearing in it as managers or players. A dwelling house is hired and then fitted up for gambling. The keeper establishes a shop in the front facing the street, and constructs a passage on one side of it leading to the back of the premises. In some houses the shop communicates by a door at the back with the passage. At the end of this passage a door is placed which leads into a second passage, running in the opposite direction to the first; at the end of the second passage is a door which leads into a third passage, running the whole length of the house, at the end of which is the fourth door which leads into the gambling room; these doors are secured by several wooden bolts, and at each a watchman is placed. It has sometimes happened that the keeper of the last door, on the alarm being given that the police was at hand has secured his door and enclosed the other door keepers in the passages, where they have been found by the police. At the outer door a sentinel is placed who gives the alarm by calling out a few words announcing the arrival of the police. The principal game is called "poh". It is played with a die which is placed in a brass box and kept from moving by a smaller box which fits into the first. At the bottom of the inner box is an iron pin, the end of which rests on the die and keeps it from turning. The keeper of the gaming house holds the "poh," puts into a red bag, places the die in it and slides the inner box on it. A mat marked with a diagonal cross is placed on the floor or on a low table in the centre of which he twists the "poh" when it loses its motion the die is uncovered. The six sides of the die are equally divided and painted red and white; the players stake at the two legs of the cross facing the poh holders and between them. When the die is uncovered the players opposite the red side are winners. Each winner pays a percentage to the bank which is divided by the owners of the gaming-house. The amount of the stakes and the rules of the game vary. The bank is generally kept in an upper room to clear of bad characters. A scuffle is sometimes provoked by these fellows and as much money as the keeper has by him is stolen during the *fracas*. To save the bulk of the money therefore, it is kept in the upper room, and the banker is supplied with money as it is wanted through a trap door in the floor above in a basket. A trap door is also fixed above the stairs which is always well secured by stout bolts to prevent disappointed gamblers from rushing upstairs to the bank and looting it. "Poh" is said to be a very fair game, but poh boxes are made with false bottoms which can be opened so as to admit the die, when it is turned by a spring at the will of the holders of the "poh". This is the only game at which large sums are staked. On some nights a great deal of money is lost and won. Cards are played at some houses but the stakes are low; women are much given to card playing. Boys play at a game called Chumpleh which resembles Heads and Tails. The game of Wah Way, a lottery, is indulged in by all classes in Singapore to a fearful extent. Thirty six different animals, may be staked on and the prize is thirty times the amount of the stake. The "Wah Way" is supposed to be drawn at Johore where the principal office is, having branch offices in all parts of the town where the player pays his stake in with a piece of paper containing the name of the animal or other thing he stakes on, and the amount of the stake he ventures on each. About three o'clock in the afternoon whatever is the winning object out of the thirty six is announced in the town, and then lucky ones who have staked on it are punctually paid at the branch offices. The owners of the lottery having so many chances in their favor must make a great deal of money each day. Women are the principal supporters of this game, and it is said many ruin themselves and their husbands by staking all the money they can get hold of at these "Wah Way" offices. Stringent laws have been passed against illicit gaming and lotteries but without effect. In Johore and the Native States bordering on the several settlements of the Colony gaming is permitted; the Rajahs gaining a considerable revenue from the vice. Many of our Chinese merchants in Singapore, Penang and Malacca, afraid of gaming within the limits of the Colony go beyond and play to their hearts' content. Some are known to have acquired their fortunes by gaming, whilst others have been ruined. The following extract from the Penal Code of China concerning gambling was embodied in an order issued by Raffles in 1823 prohibiting gaming houses and cockpits in Singapore. "Whosoever games for money or goods shall receive eighty blows with a cudgel on the breech and all the money or property staked shall be forfeited to Government. He who opens the gambling house although he does not gamble, shall suffer the same punishment and the gaming house shall be confiscated. If Government officers gamble, their punishment shall be increased one degree." A subsequent clause enacts that "whoever gambles whether soldiers or people, shall wear the broad heavy wooden collar one month and be cudgelled with one hundred blows. Those who set up an occasional gambling house and harbour gamblers (if not numerous) shall be punished by wearing the wooden collar three months." In some cases the parties are to be transported. Gambling was some years ago legalized in Singapore and a Gambling Farm established but it was soon presented by the Grand Jury as a nuisance and suppressed. There are still amongst us a few gentlemen who are in favor of the Gaming Farm, and would re-establish it did it lay in their power to do so. Prostitution has been legalized and the government exercise a paternal control over the unfortunate creatures who are brought here from China to carry on their degraded calling; why should not, the advocates of the Gaming Farm say, the sister vice be placed under similar control.

THE GAME OF POH

POH AND MAT

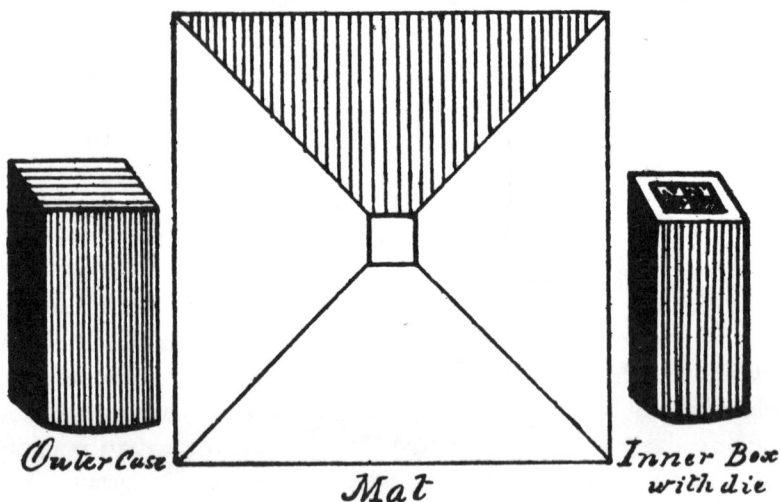

Outer Case   Mat   Inner Box
                                  with die

The die painted red and white on each side

The keeper of the poh sits on the upper part of the mat and spins the "poh" in the centre of the mat; the players sit round and stake; when the poh stops spinning the outer box is taken off and those who have staked on the side opposite the red part of the die, wins. The banker wins when the red part stops opposite the shaded part of the picture. It is an exceedingly fair game.

WHAWAY

A SPECIES OF LOTTERY

The following thirty-six animals may be staked upon:—

Cock	Lobster
Cat	Crab
Civet, or musk cat	Tiger
Tortoise	Dragon
Snake	Buffalo
Pelican	Turtle
Boa Constrictor	Rat
Pig	Lion
Duck	Dog
Frog	Leopard
Elephant	Sea Dog
Bee	Goose
Pigeon	Peacock
Swallow	Land Shell
Butterfly	Wild Duck
Fish	Horse
Deer	Monkey
Goat	Sea Serpent

The winner receives thirty times the amount of his stake.

CHINESE PLAYING CARDS

A pack of Chinese playing cards, consisting of fifty six cards, in sets of seven arranged as under.

Two sets bearing the same characters painted red; two sets painted green; two painted yellow; and two sets of white cards.

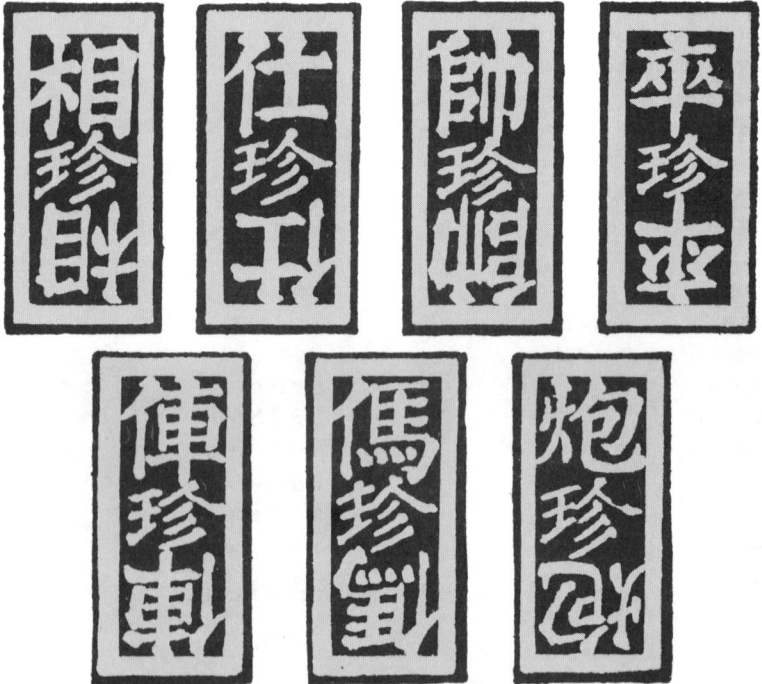

Another pack of thirty cards arranged thus:—

Another pack of playing cards consisting of one hundred and sixteen of the following patterns.

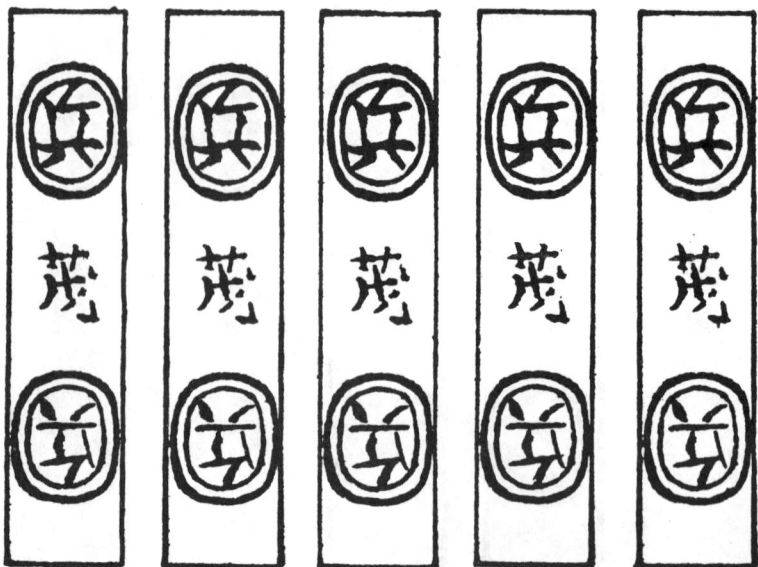

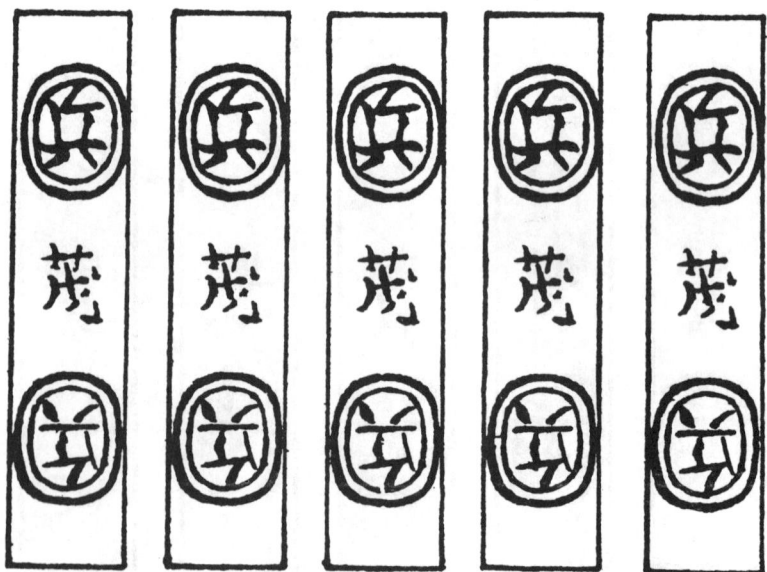

 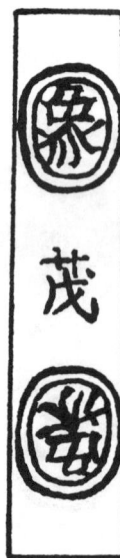 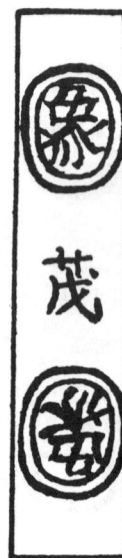 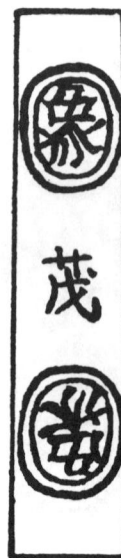

THE DRAMA

The Chinese are ardent admirers of the drama and will night after night sit to see what appears to us unmeaning spectacles. Theatrical performances consist of endless processions of soldiers, relieved occasionally by single combats of the most ludicrous nature. The dresses are gorgeous; long silk gowns covered with designs of dragons and flowers and quaint devices worked with gold thread. These dresses cost a great deal of money. There appears to be no definite plot in their dramas which are said to be representations of events that occurred during the Ming or native dynasty; but what the story is no Chinaman in the Straits appears to know; the writer has never met one that understood the dialect that the actors speak in, and half a dozen spectators will give a totally different version of the play.

Their domestic plays however are more intelligible and are replete with fun. The Chinese are splendid comic actors; their by-play is most expressive, their pantomine so good that one has no difficulty to understand the plot of these plays. The comic actors are equal to the best actors on the London stage. The writer has enjoyed as hearty a laugh at a Chinese theatre as in London with Buckstone or other comedian on the stage. Between the acts or scenes of the historical plays a company of acrobats is invariably introduced to amuse the audience. These are far inferior to European athletes. The summersaults are difficult seeing that they are always done without a spring board.

There is no scenery, and no orchestra beyond half a dozen fellows who sit on the stage and during the whole performance keep up an incessant din with flageolets, cymbals, gongs and wooden clappers. During the domestic dramas the music is somewhat modified, and sometimes a vocal solo is indulged in which has not the faintest shadow of a melody about it. The absence of scenery is made up by appropriate bits of furniture being placed on the stage to give the spectators some idea of what the scene is supposed to be. In Shakespeare's days a board was thrust on to the stage from the wing with "a wood," or "a cottage" or "a tavern" written on it to enlighten the audience.

There are no female performers. Women are represented by young men who play their parts capitally deceiving the Chinese themselves. The writer has been at plays where some of the spectators have declared some of the performers to be women, but he has been assured by the

[85]

proprietors of the theatre that women are not admitted into their companies.

The theatres are simply large barns with a stage erected at one end; with a screen running across the stage about twenty feet from the front with two doors, for the exits and entrances of the actors. Rough seats are provided for the audience and charges of admission vary from twenty five cents to half a dollar. During the performance the audience smoke and chat away at the top of their voices; when anything interesting is going on they sit very still and pay great attention to the stage. Europeans sometimes make up parties to visit the theatre, when it is advisable to request the manager to omit scenes that are treated with indifference by the Chinese but are indecent in the extreme.

The faces of the heroes of the play are usually painted white with black stripes; or black with white stripes; and the comic man is distinguished by a red or blue nose. The latter's sallies are always greeted with bursts of laughter, though as observed before not a word of his language is understood. There are theatres in Singapore occupied by Macao, Tay Chew, and Hokien actors. Besides these fixed companies there are itinerant companies who perform on hastily erected stages before audiences who stand in the open air unsheltered from wind and rain.

There are also companies of boy actors, who dress like their seniors and perform similar plays. Besides living actors there are exhibitions of puppets or marionettes which are decked out like living actors and go through the same plays. To a European one or two visits to the theatre suffice for a lifetime. The din, smoke, and foul air within are somewhat too much for his sensibilities. The writer first witnessed a Chinese performance in Penang in 1853 and wrote the following letter to the *Penang Gazette* on the subject:—

"Curiosity led me last night to visit our Theatre Royal. At first I was inclined to feel disgusted with the noise and unmeaning processions, and was about to leave but as the manager asserted that the jumping would soon follow, I remained in the lobby enjoying a manila when a shout of applause from the Chinese portion of the audience drew my attention to the stage, and with the assistance of a celestial friend I caught the meaning of the actors. The scenes that followed I think you will allow deserve to be classed with our best farces. The characters were well

[86]

sustained and the part of the young huntsman, Mah Gwan, well played by the boy. In the first scene after meeting the princess in the forest as described in the hand bill, he comes before his father who rates him for his inattention to his books, and fondness for hunting; the young man ridicules the old one who is so exasperated that he endeavours to chastise the lad; the latter in the struggle pushes the old man rather roughly which causes him to fall into a chair and faint; the by play here is splendid. Mah Gwan is delighted at his success and boasts of having defeated the old man with a slight push; he then tries to revive him by blowing on his face; his cautious approach, the comic leer, and the hasty retreat after blowing, were equal to Buckstone or Oxberry; he is then emboldened to pull the old man's nose but nothing restores him; the mother meanwhile upbraids him for his ingratitude and slyly intimates that the father may have been killed by his rough treatment. The sudden transition from exuberant mirth to excessive grief was first rate; the lad weeps, falls on his knees before his father and bows his head to the ground completely off his guard—the wily old gentleman, who has been feigning, throws a scarf round the lad's neck and has him buckled to a block of stone; and leaves him with a book; the lad endeavours to learn, but soon gives it up in disgust, and casts the book aside; he then finds the stone lighter than he imagined and walks off with it on his shoulder. In the next scene he is sitting alone quite disconsolate and hungry—one of his father's domestics, a comic fellow too, brings in some rice in a pail for his dinner—all this is capital—the servant's laugh at seeing him so dull —his description of the father's dinner which works the lad into a terrible rage—the recital of the deeds of a gallant soldier who has been named "the greatest general of his age;" and his horror at the young man's escape, who slips the stone off and takes the opportunity of bolting, while he is kow-towing; this with Mah Gwan's acting was ludicrous in the extreme. The scenes that follow are tragical and are described in the play bill,—they incline too much to the burlesque to please described ideas. At the close of the play the whole "Corps dramatique" performed a series of gymnastic tricks of a surprising nature. They are beyond my descriptive powers—and must be seen to be admired. From what I saw last night I am of opinion that the the Chinese are excellent comic actors.

July 8th, 1853."

CLANNISHNESS

The Chinese regard all people bearing the same surname as brothers and sisters, and carry the absurdity to such an extent that a man may not marry a woman of the same clan, though he may be a native of the south of China and she of the extreme north, and it is certain that they could not possibly be related. Moreover it is a common practice for childless people to adopt the children of others, it matters not of what clan, and these have to assume the surname of their adopted fathers. There is scarcely a family in the Straits that has not adopted children within its circle. Foster brothers and sisters treat each other with as much love and affection as do real brothers and sisters.

Their clannishness leads to dire results. If a quarrel arises between a man of one clan with one of another the members of their respective clans adopt the quarrel and fight to the death in support of their brethren. Many of the riots that have occurred in the Straits have been caused by disputes between rival clans. Sir John Davis says "The attention bestowed by the Chinese on their deceased ancestors, and the prevalence of clanships, or extensive societies claiming a common descent, give to the lower orders some of the feeling which in England belongs only to persons of family, but which has characterized the Scotch people very generally. The natives of Canton province and of Fokien are the most remarkable in China of the extent to which this feeling of clanship is carried, and for the inconveniences to which it gives rise. In Fokien two clans fell out in this manner in 1817. The name of one was Tsae, and of the other Wang, and a gathering of each having taken place, they fought till many were killed and a number of houses destroyed by fire. The police seized the most violent; but the worsted clan again attacked the other, and killed several of them until the Government called out the military to restore order. The Chinese even carry this feeling abroad with them. Their skill as cultivators had occasioned some hundreds to be employed at St. Helena, and when Sir Hudson Lowe was Governor of that island, he informed the writer that two clans from different provinces of China having quarrelled in 1819 met together to have a battle royal. A sergeants' party turned out to quell the disturbance; but the stronger side, running up the side of one of the steep ravines, began to roll down stones, while the weaker one joined the soldiers, who were at length compelled to fire in their own defence by which several Chinese were killed, and order soon restored."

EDUCATION

The Chinese are keenly alive to the benefits of a good education and every man of any means has a teacher for his children residing on the premises, who daily imparts the knowledge of Chinese classics to his pupils. The poor do their utmost to save enough out of their hard earnings to maintain their children at the schools established in the Colony under the protection of Government, where a good English education is provided at a very little expense to the general public. Chinese is also taught in these schools. The Chinese have also day schools of their own where their own language is taught. In Singapore the Hokiens have an excellent school, where two teachers have about one hundred boys in attendance daily. Their system of teaching is extraordinary. The pupils learn by heart in a loud voice; although each may be at a different book. In the midst of this babel of voices the master hears one boy repeat his lesson; the latter stands with his face to the wall to distract his attention from the other boys and yells out the words at the top of his voice. Several books are thus taught and when they are committed to memory the meaning of the symbols or characters are imparted.

The majority of *Babas* however have abandoned the study of the Chinese language, and confine their attention to English. Few of the rising generation are taught Chinese and doubtless in a decade or two English will supersede the Chinese language altogether. With reference to the spoken language the *Babas,* especially those of Malacca, so interlard their conversation with Malay words and sentences that, it is difficult sometimes to say whether they are speaking Chinese or Malay. The result is very ludicrous. The writer, who knows a little of the Hokien dialect, has often enjoyed a hearty laugh whilst listening to a set of Hokien *Babas* conversing with each other in what they call Chinese. Many *Babas* abandon the Chinese altogether and only converse in Malay.

What an extraordinary language is that of China. A distinct language is spoken in each province, quite unintelligible to the inhabitants of the adjoining provinces, and yet the written language is understood by every man in the vast empire who can read. The written language is a monosyllabic language of symbols; each character representing a certain abstract idea, or tangible object, and nothing else. They have no alphabet, no grammar to puzzle the student. It may be called a picture language. The symbol of a horse represents a horse to every educated Chinaman, as well as to the Coreans, Hylams, natives of Formosa, Cochin Chinese, and Cambodians; it is called *Mah* in Canton; *Bay* in Amoy and a thousand other names in the several places. So the symbol presenting a man is called *Lang* in one place, *Jin* in another and so on. But the symbols representing a horse and a man cannot be mistaken for any thing else, and so of all the other symbols.

Chinese words are incapable of any modification of form. Their meaning is often ascertained by their position in a sentence. The same word is at one time an adjective; at another, a substantive; and again a verb, or an adverb.

Dr. Williams says of the Chinese language. "This peculiarity of the Chinese language—that of having many sounds for the same symbols like the different names of the Arabic numerals among European nations, probably at first attached also to the Egyptian symbols; but the phonetic element there triumphed at last over the symbolic, and the Egyptian became finally an alphabetic language. Not so with the Chinese written language; this still maintains its ideographic character, and is now used as the written medium for the intercourse of more human beings than any other. The forms and significances of the symbols, too, have altered so slightly that inscriptions a thousand years old are read without difficulty and books written thirty centuries ago are daily quoted as good authority both for style and for precept."

During the China war of 1841-42 the writer was a midshipman on board of one of the East India Company's men of war belonging to the Bengal Marine and the captain of this vessel had no difficulty in conversing with the natives wherever he went, through the intervention of the Chinese carpenter, picked up at Singapore, chiefly for his knowledge of the written language of China.

It used to be very amusing to see the attempts he made to make his countrymen understand him when he spoke of them in his own vernacular, his tail and Chinese attire; but as soon as a black board made for the purpose was produced and he wrote a few cabalistic figures upon it, he was at once understood and greeted as a friend, and plentiful supplies of provisions followed his communications.

The said Captain did an exceedingly bold act with impunity in the Yang-tse-Kiang in the very height of the war, a few days after the capture of the city of Ching-Kiang-Foo, all owing to the presence of the Chinese carpenter. He went up to a town situated on the banks of a river, or canal, that flowed into the great stream, with two boats armed with twenty or thirty men each, with a brass three pounder at the bow. The writer was in one of the boats. On nearing the town an alarm was given of our approach, gongs were beaten, and when the town appeared we saw hundreds of Chinese on the banks, including soldiers ready to receive us. In our leading cutter the Captain sat with two officers, and at the bow the Chinese carpenter stood holding up the black board written over with chalk in Chinese characters, expressing good will to the people and friendship, and further that we wished to communicate with the Governor of the Town. On reaching the landing place we disembarked without opposition, and shortly after, the interpreter had made our wishes known, through his magic slate, down came a mandarin and several followers. We said all we wanted were provisions and were prepared to pay liberally for the same; holding up a few dollars to convince them. The almighty dollar had its charm; in half an hour or so, we got all we wanted, and during our stay were treated with the greatest civility and kindness, although we were surrounded with armed soldiers, who must have heard of the victories on the Yang-tse-Kiang, and who could in a few minutes by dint of numbers alone have killed our small party or made us prisoners.

About this time the Chinese had captured several of our countrymen and had gained some *eclat* by showing them about the country in cages; others they decapitated and sent their heads to Pekin. Few men would have ventured so fearlessly into the very clutches of an armed foe within a few miles of a captured city with war raging all around; and strange to say we came away unharmed and not an angry face was to be seen amongst the crowds of men who flocked out of the gate of the town to see us.

A table and chairs were brought, and the elders of the city sat and had a most interesting conversation with us through the invaluable carpenter. It was a curious sight to see the skipper sitting as cool as a cucumber smoking his cigar surrounded by our foes.

The writer can testify to the kindness of the common people during this war, as it is called the opium war. He has landed on the banks of the great river Yang-tse-Kiang and gone up to small farm houses and been hospitably treated by the inmates. Nothing struck him more than the cleanliness of these country people and the English air about their houses; in the kitchens especially; floors well swept; dishes, pans, and plates neatly arranged on shelves, with chairs and tables of clumsy make but homely; such a striking contrast to the homes of other Asiatics. The Chinese are the only people of Asia who use chairs and tables. In the bed rooms were bedsteads, tables, chairs, pictures, stands with ornaments, and other pieces of furniture resembling those of English houses.

Since writing the above the writer has found in Dr. Williams' introduction to his last Chinese dictionary the following remarks which account for the natives on the bank of the Yangtse not understanding the Chinese carpenter, who must have been ignorant of the mandarin dialect although he knew the written language of China. Had he known the court dialect he could have conversed freely with the natives for Dr. Williams says "The speech of the great body of the educated classes among the Chinese, called by them the *Kwan Hea* or official language, and known as the court or mandarin dialect is spoken throughout the regions north of the Yangtse river without much variation in its idiom and grammatical construction, and very extensively in the provinces north of it, except in Fuhkien and Kwantung to such a degree as to make it the prevailing speech in sixteen of the provinces."

JUDICIAL OATHS

All superstitious oaths were some years ago abolished in this Colony by the Legislative Council of India, and in lieu thereof a simple affirmation was substituted, the witness holding up his right hand on high and saying that he will speak the truth, and nothing but the truth so help his God. The Chinese consider no oath binding on their consciences unless they cut a cock's head off, or burn sacrificial paper, or let a saucer fall on the floor and shiver to pieces; each form is emblematical of the dire end the operator is sure to meet with if he tells a lie.

The scene in our Courts of law are sometimes exceedingly laughable. A raw Chinese gets into the witness box and is told by the Interpreter to hold his hand up, witness incontinently holds up his left hand, Interpreter "the other hand." Up goes the right hand whilst the left is still up. Interpreter, "no, no, not both hands;" down go both arms. Interpreter "hold up your right arm." Up goes the left; and so on over and over again; the audience in the meanwhile being convulsed with laughter. Repeated trials are made to get witness to do what is required. Magistrate and Interpreter lose their tempers, the witness gets more and more flurried, and sometimes many minutes elapse before the slightest idea of what is wanted seems to dawn on his mind. At length the Interpreter is forced to hold the man's arm up and endeavour to make him repeat like a parrot the words of the oath.

This is nearly as difficult a job as to get him to hold the right hand up; has not the slightest idea as to the meaning of the formula and several minutes elapse before he can be got to repeat it. Sometimes, after repeated trials, when the patience of all present is exhausted threatening is tried which further obfuscates the man; at length when all are in despair, he appears to awaken suddenly to what is required of him; holds up his proper hand and repeats the words after the Interpreter glibly enough much to the disappointment of the Chinese portion of the assembly who are highly tickled and anticipate further fun.

The Interpreter in the meanwhile venting his ill-humour on the unfortunate wretch in the choicest celestial Billingsgate. Such scenes are disgraceful and might be avoided by abolishing all oaths and punishing witnesses for speaking untruths as severely as if they uttered them under the sanction of an oath. After a life long experience, the writer is satisfied that judicial oaths have very little effect upon people in general whatever their nationality may be. An habitual liar will tell a falsehood in spite of any oath; whilst on the other hand the truthful man does not require the sanctity of an oath to aid him to state what is true.

SUPERSTITIONS

The Chinese people nooks, corner of roads, trees, rocks and sundry other places with fays and fairies and goblins damned inumerable, and do them worship to propitiate them. Incense sticks, slips of paper, tinsel ornaments and other gewgaws may be seen at the most out of the way spots showing that the inhabitants of the neighbourhood have discovered an evil spirit there-abouts.

Silk cotton trees have invariably a female demon, called *Hantu Pontianak*. These creatures assume the loveliest female shapes, and appear on the high roads, especially on moonlight nights and allure men to their destruction. They are exercised by driving a few long iron nails into the tree. If a nail is driven into this goblin's head she immediately becomes human. They sometimes appear at feasts and eat and drink and enjoy themselves like other people, and win the hearts of the young men.

Hantu, goblin, spectre,—*Crawfurd.*

There is a legend that, in Malacca once, a young fellow fell in love with one of these goblins at a feast, and knowing her to be a *hantu* got an iron nail and a hammer and suddenly drove the former into her skull, and she at once became a real woman ànd married the young man. They had a son, and years after the goblin having grown tired of her human existence told her son to feel in her hair that something had got there troubling her; he did so and came upon the head of the iron nail that his father had driven in; his mother told him to pull it out, he did so and immediately to his astonishment the mother vanished through the roof and was never seen again.

There is another demon, very tall and ghastly called *Hantu Gallah,* he waylays men in out of the way places and takes their heads off. There is one goblin who only has a head and no body, a cherub perhaps, who also waylays men and destroys them.

If a man is very ill and other modes fail to cure him, he makes an image like himself in paper, and puts it with some money and food in a paper house and places it in a tree and the evil spirit that is punishing him it is supposed will be appeased.

Nor is the belief in demons confined to the lowest classes; in the garden of one of the richest men in Singapore at Pasir Panjang may be seen an immense granite boulder supposed to be the abode of evil spirits, enshrined in a handsome temple in which worship is held to appease the demons. They have a strong belief in persons being possessed with devils. At some of the country temples sometimes dwells a demoniac or two, and they are consulted by sick persons. A *Baba* told the writer that he was very ill some years ago with dysentery and all the Chinese doctors in Town, Singapore, failed to cure him; he was advised to visit one of these demoniacs on the Geylang Road, which he did; the impostor received him with great ceremony and suddenly began to shake all over as if moved by some spirit and he then directed the inquirer to do a lot of nonsensical things which he said would cure him. The *Baba* tried the remedies but without success, and eventually appealed to an English doctor, who successfully cured him; so much for science. The *Baba's* faith in the possessed has ever since been much shaken.

This man has a strong belief in the return of the spirits of the dead to the earth, he says that if he is tardy in the 3rd and 7th moons to prepare the sacrifices for the benefit of his departed ancestors the spirit of his father appears to him at night and upbraids him for his undutiful conduct; and he there and then gets out of bed and slaughters fowls and ducks to satisfy the old gentleman.

Nearly every disease a man gets is assigned to the malignity of evil spirits. If the worship of the dead is neglected or improperly performed the spirits are sure to punish the living. To counteract the influence of evil *Babas* hang up in their houses sprigs of certain plants, one called *jaringo* and another of the aloes kind; or they nail over the door a picture of a god or goddess; the *Tae Keih or patpah** as it is called by the *Babas* is also put up for good luck.

Babas believe in the use of many Malay charms and tie them on their arms, or hang them around their necks. The belief in the *Ubat gunah* a spell or charm that wins the heart of a man or woman in spite of all obstacles, is universal; they also believe that the red slips of paper which they buy from fortune tellers written over with Chinese characters pasted up on the door posts of a house keep away evil spirits. Jade stones are worn as charms, these are supposed to wax whiter when the wearer is about to be unlucky, or reddish when he is to be prosperous; similar to the superstitious belief that coral beads change color as the health of the wearer varies.

SECRET SOCIETIES

Secret societies abound in the Straits. They are the offspring of the famous Triad society of China; meaning "the society of the three united, Heaven Earth and Man," which according to Chinese philosophy says Davis imply the three departments of nature. The Triad society it is said was formed for the patriotic object of expelling the Manchus and restoring the native or Ming Dynasty. It is known in the Straits Settlements, as the "Ghi Hin or Tian Tay Hoey or Kongsi" literally. "The Heaven and Earth Society," and amongst the members are enrolled Malays, Klings and other classes as well as Chinese. It is said that some Europeans on the first settlement of Singapore, who lived far away from the Town beyond the protection of the police joined the society for protection.

Mr. Pickering in an interesting article on the Chinese in the Straits published in August 1876 in Fraser's Magazine, states that the great Tai Ping rebellion mainly owed its origin and certainly much of its

Vide page 50.

strength and ferocity to the Traid Society. The writer was so informed by the Chinese of Penang at the out-break of the rebellion as stated in his previous paper published in the Journal of the Indian Archipelago. Davis in his work on the Chinese, upon the authority of Dr. Milne who had taken great pains to investigate the nature and objects of the Triad society, states that "in the reign of Kea King, about the commencement of the present century, the Triad society under another name, spread itself rapidly through the provinces and nearly succeeded in overturning the Government. In 1803 its machinations were frustrated, and the principal leaders seized and put to death, the official reports stating to the Emperor that not a single member of that rebellious fraternity was left alive. But the fact was otherwise, for they still existed, and with a view to secrecy adopted the name which they at present bear.

The objects of the association appear at first to have been allied to something like freemasonry and to have aimed simply at mutual aid and assistance; but as the number increased, their views degenerated from the laudable ends of reciprocal benefit to robbery, violence and the overthrow of Government; and the acquisition of political power by the expulsion of the Tartar Dynasty.

The management of the combination is vested in three persons who are denominated *Ho* "elder brethren" in the same manner that freemasons call themselves "brothers." The society's regulations are said to be written for greater security on cloth, which on any emergency may be thrown into a well, or otherwise concealed for a time.

The ceremony of initiation is said to take place at night. The oath of secrecy is taken before an idol and a sum of money given to support the general expense. There is likewise a ceremony called "Kuo-Keaou" passing the bridge," which bridge is formed by swords, either laid between two tables, or else set upon the hilts and meeting at the points in form of an arch.

The persons who receive the oaths take it under this bridge and the *Ye Ko* or chief brother reads the articles of the oaths to each of which an affirmative response is given by the new member after which he cuts off the head of a cock, which is the usual form of a Chinese oath intimating, thus perish all who divulge the secret.

Some of the marks by which they make themselves known to each other consist of mystical numbers of which the chief is the number three. Certain motions of the fingers constitute a class of signs. To discover if

[96]

one of the fraternity is in company, a brother will take up his tea cup, or its cover, in a particular way with three fingers and this will be answered by a corresponding sign.

They have a common seal, consisting of a pentagonal figure, in which are inscribed certain characters in a sense understood only by the initiated.

Except in their dangerous or dishonest principles the Triad society or *San-ho-hoey* bear a considerable resemblance to the society of freemasons. They even pretend to carry their origin back to remote antiquity under another name. The members swear at their initiation to be fraternal and benevolent which corresponds with the engagement of the freemasons. Another point of resemblance is in the ceremonies of initiation, in the oath and the solemnity of its administration. Dr. Milne observes that the signs, particularly the use of fingers, as far as known or conjectured, appear to bear a resemblance. Some have affirmed that the great secret of freemasonry consists in the words "liberty and equality;" and if so certainly the term *heung ti* "brethren" of the Triad society may be explained as implying the same idea".

The descriptions given to the writer as set out in the following pages by members entering the Ho Seng Society in Penang correspond in many particulars with the account given by Dr. Milne. The following legend connected with the origin of the Triad society was related to the writer at Penang. "Some hundreds of years ago the Emperor of China was so beset by his enemies that he despaired of his life and kingdom; hearing that there were three hundred priests famous for their valor and skill in magic, he appealed to them for assistance which was readily granted. The priests alone defeated all the armies that opposed the Emperor and restored him to his former greatness. Finding himself free of his enemies, the perfidious monarch instead of being grateful to his deliverers, conceived the greatest mistrust of them; before an assembly of his ministers he stated that if the priests were so powerful as to defeat such vast armies, they might turn their arms against himself, therefore, the best plan would be to kill them by stratagem.

He managed to destroy all but three, (five more correctly), who settled in different parts of the kingdom Quangtung, Fukien and other provinces". The escape of the five priests was thus graphically described to the writer by one of the elder brethren of the society in Singapore; "on reaching a wide river with the King and his army in full chase their protecting genu threw a magic bridge across for them to escape in safety, which remained long enough to let the greater part of the pursuing host pass over to within a few yards of the opposite bank, when it disappeared with a fearful noise letting their enemies sink into the roaring flood beneath to perish as they deserved." The names of the five priests were as the writer is informed by Mr. Pickering, Aw-tek-te, Png-tai-hong, Choa-tek-tiong, Ma-chiou-hin, and Lee-sek-khan.

They collected a few friends around them and established these secret societies for their mutual protection and with the object of hurling from the throne the Emperor and his dynasty in retaliation for his ungrateful conduct. Before the priests separated, they agreed upon the rules and signs of the intended secret societies. Mr. Pickering says in Fraser that the mandarins of China while often conniving at clan feuds and using them as excuses for extortion, crush with a vigorous hand, when discovered, any attempt to form a secret society; even to belong to one is a capital offence. The Chinese Government know by sad experience what powerful engines the Hoeys are against any settled rule or good order.

In this Colony the Triad society has no political object, but was established for laudable purposes. The Ghi Hin Hoey or society was introduced into Singapore by members of that society from Penang and Johore, and into Penang and Malacca from China, and until the original society was divided into rival branches the writer is of opinion that it worked a great deal of good; and to this day much of the peace that exists in the Colony is due to the influence of the secret societies.

Mr. Pickering writes in the article already referred to: "The Chinese emmigrants to the Straits consists for the most part, of the lowest classes of the population of the two most *turbulent* provinces of China, Kwangtung and Fuhkien. The miners and artisans are from the former province, and belong to two distinct tribes speaking different dialects, viz., the Puntis or Macaos, and Hakkas or Khehs: these two tribes have been at enmity in China for years. The agriculturists, boatmen and small shopkeepers come from the districts around Chu-Chao-Foo, or Tay-Chew in Quangtung, or from the province of Fuh-Keen. Tay Chews and Hokiens are often engaged in their own country in petty feuds. Every emigrant on leaving China carries with him, if nothing else, the prejudice of race or the remembrance of his clan or district feud; these are elements of discord in any mixed Chinese community, but small compared with the baneful influences of the Heaven and Earth societies for the interests of which the Chinese is obliged and willing to forget his family, clan and district."

The writer is of a different opinion; it seems to him that, a society enfolding the whole of these discordant elements within its embrace, and binding these hereditary enemies together under the most solemn vows of brotherhood and kinship, much of the ill-feeling brought from China would be dissipated and expelled. And such was the indisputable fact, and to a great extent the influence of these societies exercise a similar effect to this day; unfortunately from the original society splitting up into a dozen rival societies more elements of discord it is true are introduced amongst the Chinese, but not in the light of those who place all the discord amongst them at the doors of the secret societies. It is a popular error that most of the riots that have from time to time disturbed the peace of this Colony originated with the secret societies; such is not the case, the greatest riot we ever had in Singapore viz., that of 1854 occurred between the natives of Fuhkien and Kwangtung. The former under the generic term *Hokiens* were ranged against four races on the other side, viz., the *Macaos, Kehs, Tay Chews,* and *Hylams*. The solemn obligations of the secret societies were cast to the winds, and members of the same Hoey fought to the death against their brethren. In 1870-71 and again in 1872 the riots were between the Hokiens and Tay Chews; and so in 1876.

In 1854 the riots were not suppressed until martial law was proclaimed after the lives of thousands of men, women and children were sacrificed and a vast deal of property destroyed.

In 1871 troops were called out immediately the riot broke out and had a most salutary effect on the Chinese population. The whole affair was virtually over in a day, but the fact of the soldiers having been called out so quickly has done much to preserve the peace of the town since.

In 1876 the riots was also between Hokiens and Tay Chews but was quickly suppressed through the intervention of the headmen of those tribes.

Riots have occurred frequently between the great clans of Tans and Lims; the Lees and Choas; the Gohs and Hohs; the Lees and Tans; the Pohs and Choas; and between other clans. In all these disturbances the vows of the secret societies were sacrificed to the claims of family and district feuds.

The secret societies are additional elements of discord it is true, but so are any new elements introduced amongst such an inflammable population.

The Chinese converts to Christianity, Roman Catholics, regard themselves as a distinct brotherhood; they are called *Hong Kahs* and any quarrel occurring amongst their members and outsiders is at once adopted by the whole body and riots ensue. We have had disturbances between the *Hong Kahs* and Ghi Hins; and *Hong Kahs* and Ghi Hoks. The latter was a formidable affair which lasted several days and was put down with much difficulty.

Between secret societies we have had riots between Ghi Hins and Ghi Hoks; Ghi Hocks and Ghi Soons; Ghi Hoks and Hok Mengs Ghi Hocks and Hok Heens; Ghi Hins and Hok Heens. The great riot in Penang in 1870-71 were between the Toh-peh-kongs and Ghi Hins.

In Malacca in 1875 they were between the Ghi Hins and Ghi Boos. In both these settlements there have also been disturbances between tribes and races.

To suppress certain elements of discord it would certainly be advisable to crush secret societies, but on the other hand for the same reason it would be necessary to crush the *Hong Kahs,* and put a stop to all proselytism; and insist that all distinctions of clans should be abolished on Chinese landing in the colony.

If tomorrow a host of Chinese Mahomedans were to come to the Straits a fresh element of discord would be introduced and they would soon be found fighting with other sections of the community; and so it would be with the introduction of any distinctive body of Chinese. If a vast number of Chinese were converted by the Protestant Missionaries they would there and then regard themselves as brethren and bound to help each other against all comers. This peculiar idiosyncracy of the Chinese is engendered by the strong narrow minded prejudices acquired from their birth with reference to clanships. The secret of the peacefulness that prevails amongst the Chinese in Dutch and Spanish Colonies is the fact that immigration is very much confined to one race of Chinese. In Hongkong riots are unknown chiefly because the mass of the inhabitants are Cantonese. Limit the immigration of Chinese to the Straits from one province in China and peace would be the result.

As observed before when the Ghi Hin Society existed alone it worked well; it bound together Hokiens and Cantonese as brethren and protected the weaker clans against the stronger clans like the Tans, Lims, Choas, and others.

To this day much of the quiet that reigns in the country districts of this Colony is due to the fact of the inhabitants of each district belonging to the same secret society, and not from any protection afforded by the Government or from any fear of our laws.

Mr. Pickering observes in his paper that the opinion of every respectable Chinese in the Straits Settlements is that the recognition of the Hoey or Heaven and Earth societies is a disgrace to our Government. The writer has heard many respectable Chinese say the reverse. They hold that, the Hoeys do a great deal of good, and that it would be utterly impossible to uproot them. They say the chiefs and members of the secret societies are loyal to the British Government and do their utmost to preserve the peace. It is only a few unscrupulous rascals who take advantage of their influence as chiefs of the Hoeys to squeeze certain sections of the community and exercise a degree of terrorism over women and weak people who they terrify. These do so in spite of the rules of the society and might be dealt with personally by the Government and deported to China to put a stop to their nefarious practices.

The deportation of one of the heads of a secret society in 1876 for his supposed connection with the post office riots, though as far as the writer has been able to ascertain, an innocent man, has done a vast deal of good; it has shown the heads of the secret societies that, any breach of the peace might lead to any of them being sent away from the colony to the ruin of their business and families.

The registration of the members of the secret societies also has done much good. It is a remarkable fact that in all the riots we have had the greatest respect has been shown to us. The presence of one native police man in a street has been sufficient to maintain the peace there, and in no case have the police been attacked wantonly or with intention by the Chinese. The writer only knows of one instance, in 1875 or 1876 when an *emente* took place by the Chinese against the native police for certain arbitrary proceedings on the part of the latter.

In all the riots between secret societies, or clans, or tribes, the Government authorities and Europeans in general and all other classes have been scrupulously respected, and allowed to pass unharmed through streets filled with armed parties of the opposing factions.

The friendly societies or clubs must be distinguished from the Hoeys, or secret societies from which they materially differ; they are however confounded by Europeans. These Kongsis, as they are called, are formed by men of the same town, village, or district, clan, or occupation, and are very exclusive; each club has a house for the accommodation of the sick and indigent, where they are lodged and fed, and on dying are buried at the expense of the Kongsis.

The members of the Kongsis have no oath of secrecy or signs by which they may distinguish each other. The list below furnishes particulars of some of the societies registered in Singapore. In Penang and Malacca similar societies exist; each member subscribes to the funds of the Kongsi according to his means. In each a certain number of members are annually elected trustees, who collect subscriptions and the rents of houses that may belong to them, and pay the expenses of the Kongsi.

One member is elected annually as chief or chairman of the society to whom the trustees account for the money collected by them; he is called the Loo-choo. On that day of election the members of the Kongsi meet at their house and each man's name is written on a separate piece of paper, which is rolled up tightly and placed in a box. A pair of lots is thrown up before the idol, if they fall with one flat side and one convex side uppermost three times successively, one of the papers is unrolled and the man whose name is written on it becomes the Loo-Choo for the ensuing year. In the same manner are the trustees chosen.

On the election closing, the image of the guardian deity of the Kongsi is removed from the ex-Loo-Choo's house to that of the new Chief, where it remains for twelve months.

The removal is attended with a grand procession; all the members marching in rich dresses preceded by the image which is borne on a chair carried on the shoulders of coolies, and the procession is attended by numerous coolies bearing flags and symbols. In the evening the public is gratified if the Kongsi be wealthy, with a wayang or theatre at the expense of the society. The performance lasts for several nights if the funds are rich enough.

The only religious ceremony indulged in by the Kongsis is the annual worship of the dead. To a foreigner the whole affair is got up for the purpose of feasting. The night preceding the day on which this festival is observed pigs, fowls, and ducks are killed and cooked, and a party of musicians perform for several hours at the door of the Kongsi house. Early in the morning the food, with arrack and other drinks are sent to the cemetery, and the members follow.

After the ceremony is over the members eat and drink and often gamble. On some occasions when several Kongsis meet in the country cemeteries fights ensue and severe blows are interchanged. In Penang, when the writer was there, the Sin Neng Kongsi and Hoey San Hoey quarrelled at "poh" after worshipping the dead, and several men were dangerously wounded, much property destroyed and the two societies involved themselves in a lawsuit which lasted a long period.

On these occasions robbery is rife and whole plantations are destroyed; during the quarrel above-mentioned between the Sin Neng, a powerful society of Cantonese, confined to the natives of a certain district in China, and the Hye San, a Triad Society, the members of the former fought quite as desperately as those of the latter though not united by the laws of a secret society.

In Penang a quarter of a century ago there were five secret societies, viz., the Ghi Hin, Ho Seng, Hye San, Chin Chin, and Toh-peh-kong; at present there are two other Hoeys registered there as dangerous, viz, the Hok-Hak-Seah and Choon Ghe Seah. The Ghi Hin was composed chiefly of Cantonese; the Ho Seng besides Chinese enrolled Malays, Portuguese, Klings and Jawi Pukans; Hye San were chiefly Kehs; and Toh-peh Kong were Hokiens and *Babas*. The Chin Chins were chiefly Hokiens. The Ghi Hin numbered about 15,000 members in Penang and Province Wellesley. Ho Seng from 3,000 to 5,000; Chin Chin 2,000 to 3,000; Toh-peh-kongs 3,000 to 4,000; Hye San 1,000 to 2,000; these figures are problematical. Females are not admitted into the Hoeys.

A very intelligent Malay Haji who was educated at the Protestant Free School at Penang, and was well-known at one time as a prominent member of several Hoeys, gave the writer the following particulars regarding his initiation, and the object and construction of the society he belonged to, and they are singularly in keeping with the description given by Dr. Milne in Davis' China, a book the writer did not see till long after his notes were published in the "Journal of the Indian Archipelago."

The writer asked the Haji if he was not afraid of divulging the secrets after taking an oath of fidelity. He replied "no, being a Mahomedan he did not consider the Chinese oath binding; that he was not sworn on the Koran and therefore did not care; that for three or four years he had deserted the fraternity because his chief priest considered it to be contrary to the Mahomedan religion to belong to it, and he was then expiating his former wickedness by frequently attending the mosque and implicitly obeying the injunctions of the Koran."

The punghulu's statement which follows corroborates the Haji's story in some points, and he alludes to the Haji as being the principal performer on the night of his admittance or initiation.

THE HAJI'S STORY

"On any person wishing to enter a Hoey he signifies his intentions to one of the members, who tells the chief or *Thoo-Ah-Koh* who enters his name in a book; when a sufficient number of persons are desirous of entering, a night for the initiation is fixed.

When the night arrives, the members of the Hoey assemble in the principal room or hall of their house or lodge and the candidates are placed in an adjoining apartment; each man pays twenty-five cents, and his name is entered on the register of the society. At the door leading into the hall stand two men armed with drawn swords, and dressed in rich silk gowns ornamented with divers figures of dragons, birds and other creatures. Half a dozen lighted incense sticks are given to each candidate. The candidates now advance in couples to the door of the hall in a stooping posture, their right arms bared, and if Chinese their queues opened out. On arriving at the door the following questions are put by the guards to each candidate:—

Q. What do you desire by entering the Hoey?
A. I wish to become a brother of yours.
Q. Who told you to come?
A. I came of my own accord, no one told me to come.
Q. What do you hold these joss sticks for?
A. I wish to pray and swear before the Hoey, that I wish to obey all its orders.

The candidates are then allowed to enter the hall, in which is a table spread with eatables before the presiding idol or Tokong.

A member personating a priest stands to the left of the table; the Thoah-Koh stands on the right. The second grade called Jee-Koh sit in chairs on the right. The third grade or Sam-Koh on the left. The fourth grade or ordinary members called brothers stand on either side in front.

The candidates are then brought to the head of the table and are made to worship; this is done by stooping down three or four times and raising both hands with the joss-sticks over the head; each candidate says that he will strictly obey all orders of the Hoey and will not reveal to any one what he may see or hear. The priest then takes up a large book and says, "you come here unsolicited and wish to become a brother." The priest then says "I will now read the rules of this Hoey." "You will not reveal the proceedings of our meetings to any but a brother, or steal from him; you must not seduce the wife, daughter or any female relation of a brother. You must not injure his character, or disturb his peace of mind in any way."

"If you break any of these rules, you must come before the Hoey to be punished, and on no account must you go to the police or Supreme Court; the Hoey has the power of flogging you and imposing any other punishment it pleases on you."

"If you commit any serious crime like murder, or robbery, we will have nothing to do with you; you will be dismissed from the Hoey, and no brother will receive you into his house."

"If a brother commits the most heinous crime you must not inform against him, but at the same time, you must not interfere in arresting him."

"If a guilty brother is caught by the police, you must not assist in getting him off, but should the brother be innocent, you must make every exertion to get him off."

"If you see a brother make a signal, it is your duty to answer it, if he is in need of assistance you must grant it." Many other rules exist, but the Haji had forgotten them. The priest continues, "the following signs I show you, they must not be revealed.

"If about to be assaulted in the streets, roll up the right sleeve or the right leg of your trowsers, or hold the right arm over the head with the fingers spread out."

"You will wrap your tail round the head and tuck the end in over the right ear, or at the back, having the tassel hanging down.

"If you are making a bargain with a man and wish to find out if he is a brother, push the article you are bargaining about with the back of your hand if you do not agree to the price; if you do, seize it with three fingers of the right hand."

"When you salute the *Thoo-Ah-Koh* you must touch his thumb with yours. With a *Jee-Koh* and *Sam-Koh* touch the first finger of his hand with your thumb."

"On shaking hands with a brother or fourth grade, place your thumb on the back of his hand and your first finger along the palm of his. On entering a house, if you wish to be known, put your right foot in first over the threshold and look up."

"A handkerchief placed round the neck and tied in the front with two knots, with the ends left hanging down, denotes a member of the Ghi Hin; junks on meeting at sea having a peculiar way of placing their sails and flags, so as to show what Hoey they belong to.

"After enumerating all the signs and signals which are too numerous for any person to remember, every member pricks the middle finger of the right hand and drops a little blood into a bowl of arrack and each candidate is obliged to do the same. After which every member present as well as the candidates drink out of the bowl and the candidates are saluted as brethren. Each newly initiated brother now pays a dollar and ten cents, gets a seal or chop on silk, or cloth or paper, bearing his name, and he is then entitled to all privileges of the fraternity.

THE CHOP OR SEAL OF THE GHI HIN HOEY

"The Ghi Hin and the other secret societies affiliated thereto have the same signs. Some of the new societies that are not considered branches of the Ghi Hin have a few additional signs. The members of the Toh-peh-Kong at Penang recognised each other by drawing the right hand across the mouth, and if in want of aid in a street row the right arm was held up with the fist closed and thumb pointing upward. On refusing anything push away with the open hand."

Several months after hearing the Haji's story the writer was visiting one of the country stations, and recollecting a report that all the Malays at the village had entered the Ho-Seng-Hoey he took the opportunity of questioning the Punghulu (a native officer) a highly respectable man, the son of a Haji named Haji Brunie, he having been a native of Borneo. This man left some property and a large family who were very influential.

The Punghulu without any hesitation admitted the truth of the story, and said that two or three years before, all the Mahomedan male inhabitants did enter the Ho-Seng, he being one of the number. As soon as the high priest of Penang, one Agdul Gunny, heard of it, he repaired to the spot and assembled all the Mahomedans and told them that they had all become Kaffirs by joining heathens, and if they did not recant he would close the mosque in the village, take the presiding priest away, and excommunicate them all. On this they immediately renounced the Hoey and performing the usual ceremonies were re-admitted into Islamism. The following is the Punghulu's account of his initiation, but he said it occurred so long ago, and not having visited a Hoey since, he could not furnish a detailed account of the transaction, nor could he repeat the oath or describe the signs.

THE PUNGHULU'S STORY

'With two hundred Malays or more I was persuaded to join the Ho-Seng-Hoey. On the night of our initiation we assembled in the plantation of the chief of the Hoey in this district; an attap shed was lighted up, and a table spread with food was placed before a picture; two men with naked swords stood at the entrance of the shed and held them over head in the shape of a triangle, which each candidate had to pass under; we were then sworn not to reveal any of the secrets or signs that would be communicated to us. All I can now recollect is that we were to call each other "brother." We were not to injure the wife, daughter, or any female relation or friend of a brother:

"If a false charge was bought against a brother we were to make every exertion to get him free; but if a brother was arrested on a true charge, the law was to take its course."

"If in a row and in want of assistance raise the right arm, or roll up the right sleeve or one leg of the trowsers.

"On sitting tea before a man, place three cups in a row, if he takes the middle up he is a member of the Ho-Seng-Hoey.

"The ceremony of initiation was conducted in the Chinese language which Punghulu did not undersand but Haji—conducted the business and interpreted the signs and orders." The Haji mentioned by the Punghulu was the writer's first informant whose statement is set forth above.

During the day the writer paid the chief of the Ho-Seng a visit and alluded to his having admitted the Malays into his Hoey and their subsequent recantation. He denied their having been admitted into his Hoey, but said they had formed themselves into a club to assist each other against the people of the adjoining villages, and against the attack of pirates. This was said of course to put the Punghulu who was present, off the scent. If it had been merely a local club unconnected with the Ho-Seng-Hoey it is not likely that the Haji who lived in George Town would have gone eleven miles into the country to assist in the ceremony.

The Hoeys have two great days in the year, viz: in the 3rd moon when they worship the dead; and in the 7th moon when they worship evil spirits. During the latter ceremony the members of the Hoeys assemble at their Kongsi houses in town and have a great feast.

There are no regular meetings, but when an offender is to be tried for offences against the rules of the society, notices are sent round and the members assemble. If the offender is pronounced guilty he is flogged, fined, or expelled, or punished in any way the elders judge fit.

On one occasion in Penang while a constable was on his rounds, he was alarmed on passing the Ghi Hin Hoey house, by cries issuing from the building at the same time a Chinaman rushed out followed by others. The police finding the door open went in and arrested the elders, as they sat in solenm conclave and took them to the police station. The pursued and pursuers were also arrested. The former had his head cut open and severe bruises appeared about his person. He declared before the police magistrate that the elders had nothing to do with the assault, but that persons who had beaten him were bad men and against the orders of the headmen had done so. He admitted having been before the Hoey for some misdemeanour. There was no doubt that the Hoey had ordered him to be flogged and that he managed to force his way past the door keepers. Evidence could not be procured and the chief and elders were released.

The chief of the Ghi Hin who was arrested on this occasion was a Chinese named Appoo, born in Bengal, and a watch maker by trade. He lived in Penang for over sixty years and was remarkable for his honesty and benevolence. He had a small hospital for leper and poor creatures afflicted with other diseases; in which there were generally fifteen or twenty patients at a time. He gave a great deal of money away in charity, and at his own expense buried many paupers who belonged to no Hoey or Kongsi; or who had not paid their subscriptions to their societies and were defaulters and not entitled to be buried at the expense of their societies; for this purpose he always kept a number of rough cheap coffins at hand.

He had a wonderful influence over his people. At one of the Ghi Hin festivals the writer walked to the Kongsi house at night and found crowds of Chinese assembled in the streets; opposite the Hoey; and knowing that the members of the other Hoeys were also assembled in the Town to feast, the writer thought there might be disturbances if these members of rival societies met, so he sent for Appoo and told him it would be better to send his men in-doors and keep them quiet. He immediately gave an order for them to retire and shut the gates and in a few minutes the streets were deserted, and the crowd had disappeared like magic; where a minute or two before all was noise and confusion the greatest silence prevailed. Appoo was much respected by all classes. He was readily recognised by his beaver hat, or bell topper; being the only Chinaman that wore one.

So long as the writer was in Penang in charge of the Police force there and in Province Wellesley, Appoo was of the greatest assistance. The writer can also bear testimony to the aid afforded him by the heads of all the secret societies during the five years he was in Penang; these men were well known, and were all respectable, who lived upon the most amicable terms with each other, and did their utmost to preserve the peace, and often afforded information that led to the capture of offenders belonging doubtless to rival societies; the writer always found them most eager to assist the authoritees.

The writer has been in Singapore twenty-two years, and at first, instances of persons being beaten in the Kongsi houses were brought to his notice, but for several years he has heard of no such case and believes that the elders have quite abandoned such practices. The secret societies in Penang however, it must be admitted were in the habit of aiding their members to evade the course of justice. A flagrant instance occurred there in 1853, which will serve to exemplify the manner in which this was done. In the 3rd moon of that year, about the month of April, the members of a Hoey were worshipping the dead at the Macao burial ground, a mendicant having displeased them was beaten and died from the effects of the blows. Some fellow beggers of the deceased complained to the police; the perpetrators of the deed were arrested and a coroner's jury returned a verdict of wilful murder against them. On the opening of the criminal sessions in the month of June following, not a witness was to be found. These men were beggars and had lived for several years at the cemetery subsisting on the generosity of the frequenters and were too poor to have left the island without assistance; it therefore, may be inferred, and it was so reported at the time, that the secret society brought them off and paid their passage to China. Such instances were not uncommon and at every criminal sessions cases were thrown out for want of evidence.

At that time the writer was a strong advocate for the suppression of secret societies, but after a further experience of nearly a quarter of a century he has been led to modify his opinion. As elements of discord they would be better removed, but in the first place it would be utterly impossible to suppress them; and in the next, they do some good by adjusting petty quarrels and in supporting and maintaining the sick and poor; and by the mutual support and assistance the members afford each other in the country districts. After the writer removed to Singapore in 1856 instances occurred of the secret societies conniving at the escape of criminals but a change for the better has taken place within the last ten years. During that period no instances have occurred to the writer's knowledge of witnesses being sent out of the colony and the ends of justice being frustrated by the connivance of the Hoeys; and it is no unusual occurrence at the present time (1878) for the chiefs of the secret societies to give up offenders of their own societies to the police authorities and assist materially in getting them punished. The change for the better has taken place in consequence of the registration of secret societies, and the greater surveillance they have been brought under. The secret societies in Singapore at any rate, are daily resolving themselves into, what the members profess they are, elemosynary institutions for the support and maintenance of their poorer brethren, to give the members decent burial and after death that support and maintenance to their souls which, they value more perhaps than any thing in this life. And further, helping each other in the country districts against the attack of robbers. It would doubtless be a great boon to the Chinese were secret societies suppressed: but under existing circumstances, this would be an impossibility. The best way to destroy the baneful influences of these societies would be to employ more Chinese speaking Europeans of high character in the public service to make known to the ignorant Chinese the blessings of our rule and the absurdity of trusting to the Hoeys, and their chiefs who, unless exceedingly good men, exert their influence, only to squeeze the members and get all the money they can out of them for their own gratification and excess. The appointment of Mr. Pickering a gentleman thoroughly conversant with the Chinese language, and the character of the Chinese, as Protector of the Chinese, is a step in the right direction. This gentleman has a very high mission to fulfil, and if strongly impressed with his great responsibility, must effect in a few years a beneficial change in the state of affairs.

In the present day members of Hoeys have no hesitation in appearing as witnesses in our Courts against each other. Such an event was entirely unknown a quarter of a century ago; the fear of punishment at the hands of the Hoey would have deterred the boldest. It is a good sign and shows that the influence of the secret societies is being secretly undermined. At the present time the elders of all the triad societies and of many of the friendly societies sit daily in their club houses inquiring into complaints and their decisions are implicitly obeyed.

If a member of one society complains against a member of another society reference is made to the offender's society, and every effort is made to effect an amicable arrangement, and nearly always with success. Thousands of complaints both civil and criminal are thus disposed of. Were all these complaints brought into our courts of law the staff of Magistrates and Judges would have to be doubled or trebled. From the closest inquiries the writer is satisfied that the elders of the societies registered dangerous or otherwise, do their utmost to preserve the peace; and to their influence much of the peace that prevails is due.

The greatest danger to the peace of the colony lies in the hatred that exists between the lower orders of the great tribes of Hokiens and Cantonese, who have at present no recognised leaders, but fortunately in Singapore are kept in check by the influence and good advice of such men as the Hon'ble Mr. Whampoa, Tan Kim Ching, Seah Eu Chin and his sons, Tan Beng Swee, Tan Seng Poh, and other influential men of both sections; whose advice is constantly sought by their countrymen, and who are ever ready at great sacrifice to themselves, to attend to their complaints and advise them, always in favor of peace and quietness. Doubtless in Penang and Malacca the rabble are kept in check by the same influence. One of the greatest objections the writer can urge against the secret societies is that, it gives the head men of unscrupulous characters the opportunity of establishing a reign of terror amongst the people. They have always at their command a number of *samsings* or rowdies who are ready to obey their behests to the letter. These generally take possession of the brothels; act as protectors as they say to the women; and take the opportunity of fleecing these poor creatures for the benefit of themselves and their masters. All the brothels in Singapore are under the protection of certain chiefs of various secret societies, and the inmates are forced to contribute money not only for matters relating to themselves, but as a kind of blackmail for the protection afforded them. This tax is levied not only on the women, who are however the largest contributors, but on petty shopkeepers. Many of the chiefs and officers of the secret societies subsist solely on this blackmail and the monies they can squeeze out of the peaceful inhabitants of the colony. The influence of these scoundrels can only be shaken by a counter influence exercised by the police and other authorities. The writer does not agree with Mr. Pickering that secret societies can be suppressed by legislation. This has been tried with reference to gaming and proved an utter failure; and were it to be tried with secret societies a principle of antagonism would be initiated between the Chinese and the Government which at present does not exist, and which it would be unwise to invoke.

The following secret societies at Singapore are registered as dangerous:

Ghi Hin, Tay Chew
  Do. Hokien
  Do. Macao — called   The Ghi Hin emanated
       "Kong-foo-sin"   from the Triad Society of
  Do. Hylam   China
  Do. Keh "Song Pek Kwan"

Ghi-Hok   These four are branches of the Ghi
Ghi-Kee "Kong Hok"   Hin and connected with that institu-
Hok Hin   tion; but between some and the mother
Ghi Sin   society no good feeling exists.

Hye San.
*Hin Beng Hong (This society admits men of the Seh or
*Yeat Tong Koon   clan *Tan* only.)
*Tong Ngu Hong

The three marked * are not considered dangerous. In the writer's opinion these tribal societies are quite as dangerous to the peace of the colony as the Ghi Hin. The Tan society, *Hin Beng Hong* has fought with the Lims and Lees, and is powerful enough in numbers to face any of the tribal or secret societies.

It is said that in Singapore more than forty thousand Chinese belong to the Triad Societies. The Ghi Hin claims about fourteen thousand. The Ghi Hoks number ten thousand at least; the Ghi Kee, Hok Hin, Ghi Sin and Hye San about three or four thousand each.

In Penang are registered as dangerous the following societies:—

Ghi Hin	Hye San
Toh peh-Kong	Hoh Hak Seah
Ghi Hok	Choon Ghe Seah
Hoh Seng	

In Malacca the dangerous societies are:—

Ghi Hin	Ghi Boo
Hok Beng	Hye San
Hoh Seng	

It is said that, the red and white flag societies amongst the Klings are affiliated to the triad societies; the one to the Ghi Hin and the other to the Ghi Hok; but the Klings affirm that this is untrue; they say that their societies were brought from the Coromandel Coast and have no connection with the Chinese secret societies. It is a notorious fact that throughout the Colony, Malays and Klings, and other races are members of the secret societies.

Besides these dangerous societies as they are called there are registered in Singapore, a great many friendly societies or Kongsis. The objects for which many of them are established appear childish in the extreme. It would be waste of space to give a full list of these. A few are given below with the objects of the societies as an example. In Penang and Malacca there are similar societies. Every clan, every profession, the Babas, the natives of the same district or province in China all have their societies; and although they are not triad societies some, especially the clan societies are composed of great numbers and are quite as dangerous as the triad societies; and have from time to time disturbed the peace of these settlements fighting against each other or against the triad societies; and are likely at any time on the slightest provocation to do the same.

List of some of the friendly societies registered in Singapore with the objects of each set out.

Name of the Society	Objects of the Society
Sam Teong Ong Eng, Hok Kim Lye Koeh. Seh (Clan) Tan Hoey	Mutual aid in time of sickness, to help its members in the matter of funerals, and marriages. Conduct religious ceremonies in honor of the God Sam Tiang Ong on the 16th of the 9th moon and in the honor of the God Poot Chan on the 21st of the 11th moon when the Loo-choo and 3 Towkays are changed,
Leeng Say Society.	Similar to above.
Say Lee Society.	Similar.
Say Hoh Tong or Seh (clan) Lim Kongsi.	ditto. Subscriptions from $2 to $1.
Siglap Society.	To sacrifice to Teen Kong on the 21st and 22nd of the 11th moon.
Sunghi Kranji Society.	To sacrifice to and have theatricals in honor of the God Mah Cho once a year.

There are seventy such societies registered in Singapore.

THE GHI HIN SOCIETY AT SINGAPORE

The Ghi Hin society at Singapore has a fine lodge at Rochore. It is a large upper roomed building about sixty feet wide, and one hundred and twenty feet long, with extensive kitchens on each side thirty to forty feet wide extending the whole length of the building, capable of cooking dinner for several hundred men. The following nine societies are branches of the Ghi Hin, and are intimately connected with it viz., the Ghi Hin Macao, the Ghi Hin Hokien, the Ghi Hin Tay Chew, the Ghi Hin Keh or Song Pek Kwan, the Ghi Hin Hylams, the Ghi Hok, the Ghi Kee, the Ghi Sin, and Hok Hin. No event of any importance can be carried into effect by any of these without communicating with the parent society. Such as the election of an elder brother or a sinsay, or other officer; and on the 22nd of the 7th moon, and 22nd of the 12th moon of each year, the members of all these societies feast together at this lodge. The feast costs each member about twnety to thirty cents. The main building consists on the ground floor of two large halls with an open paved court yard between them having no roof over it.

These halls are used for feasting only. The upper floor has also two large halls divided by an open square over the paved court on the ground floor. The front hall is only used on important occasions, when enquiries are made by the elders into complaints against other societies; or when a very large number of candidates are initiated; it is bare of furniture. In the principal hall or lodge, is the shrine containing the tablets of the five founders of the society named.

> AW TEK TEE
> PNG TAI HONG
> CHOAH TEK TIONG
> MA CHIOW HIN
> LEE AEK KHAN

They are usually called "Ngoh Choh" or "Go Foo;" before the shrine are tables for the incense holders. "Ngoh Choh" is said also to refer to the five races embraced by the society. The *Macaos, Kehs, Hokiens, Tay Chews,* and *Hylams.* On the right and left of the shrine are carved cabinets containing the tablets of deceased officers of the Ghi Hin with their names, and dates of death inscribed thereon in golden letters; with incense vases before them. These tablets are sacrificed to and worshipped at the proper seasons. The chop or seal of the society represented at page

106 has to be brought at the death of a deceased member to the *Sin Say* or Secretary of the society for registration, so as to entitle his names to be worshipped by the society. To receive this worship at death appears to be one of the chief objects of all Chinese in joining these secret societies. Three doors lead into the main building gaudily painted with grotesque figures; and a few harmless pictures adorn the vestibule. A couple of large Chinese lanterns hang before the entrance and a few lanterns of the same kind are hung about the building. There are complimentary boards, the presents of wealthy members of the society hung up in different places. The premises are occupied by a few indigent brethren, and is not kept in a cleanly state. The buildings are substantially built and must have cost the fraternity several thousand dollars. There are no masonic symbols about the building. The writer was informed by a *Baba*, once a member of the Ghi Hin, and now, 1878, an elder of one of the secret societies, that when initiated, he had to pass through these arches, the last guarded by two men with drawn swords; that after taking the oath that he would be faithful to the society and obey all its orders, he pricked his finger and let a few drops of blood fall into a basin of arrack; all the initiated did the same, and after the ceremony concluded every member present, as well as the newly initiated drank some of the bloody liquid, and by that ceremony all became brothers. The principal object of his society is mutual protection and assistance, and the worship of deceased members. On his initiation and at every initiation the elder brother or "Sin Seh," if present, impresses the members with the necessity of being loyal and submissive to the powers that be, and that they are to do their utmost to live quietly and peaceably; and that in the event of any brother harming another, they are immediately to bring the matter before the society and be guided by the advice of the elders and on no account are they to take the law in their own hands, and beat or ill use the offender. If the matter can be amicably settled by the society, well but if not the disputants are referred to the law courts. The informant repudiated vehemently that any secret society would teach their members to screen each other if guilty of murder or other heinous crime. He said the Ghi Hin and the society he belonged to, did their utmost to preserve the peace, and live happily under the British Government. The organization of the Ghi Hin society by this man's story appears perfect. He said that every fifty or hundred members have a chief to whom they must refer in all emergencies; over these chiefs there are elders and the

latter are under the headmen whose orders must be implicity obeyed. In his experience, he had never known in all the riots and distrubances that have taken place in Singapore, the chiefs or elders of the secret societies encourage their members to fight. But the rabble have fought in spite of the elders, who throughout the quarrel have done their utmost to restrain their people, and suppress the fighting. In every case the elders of the secret societies have forced their members to make peace. In the great riots between *Hokiens* and *Macaos* they had regard to their secret societies.

The following rules and oaths are registered by the Ghi Hok society as *bona fide* but are supposed to be manufactured for the purpose of deceiving the police authorities. This may be so, but it is a remarkable fact that, the writer has during the numerous inquiries he has made on the subject elicited from people of all classes professing to be members of the Ghi Hin society rules and oaths to a similar effect.

RULES OF THE GHI HOK SOCIETY

1. Any man wishing to join the Ghi Hok society must listen to the instructions of the headmen who teach him above all, obedience to parents.

2. Any person joining the Ghi Hok society must obey the Company's* law and the orders of the headmen; if a brother through disobedience, or inattention to the orders of the headmen gets into trouble, he must manage for himself, as the society will have nothing to do with it.

3. Any member of the Ghi Hok society being about to marry if he will apply to the headmen of the society they will present him with the sum of $4.

4. Any members of the Ghi Hok society illicitly making or dealing in *Chandu* if arrested by the Police must manage the affair himself as the headmen of the society will have nothing to do with it.

5. Any member of the Ghi Hok society illicitly making or dealing in spirits, if he is arrested by the Police must manage the affair himself as the headmen of the society will have nothing to do with it.

6. Any member of the Ghi Hok society dying and leaving a wife or children here without means of subsistence if they come and acquaint the headmen they will receive the sum of $1 and 50 catties of white rice.

7. A member of the Ghi Hok society dying and leaving behind wife and child if he marry again and desert the child the headmen of the society on being made acquainted with the fact will support the child till he be grown up and thus keep up the posterity of their brother.

*Company—Govermnent.

8.   If the concubine of a member of the Ghi Hok society run away with another man, he must not secretly call the brethren to come forward and break the laws by fighting it is his own business and he must manage it; the headmen will not interfere. If his lawful wife run away with another man he should acquaint the headmen and if he has no money to take proceedings in the Court, they will provide him with a sufficient sum to take out a summon and so let the Government punish the offender.

9.   Any member of the Ghi Hok habitually quarrelling and fighting or abusing people, if he will not listen to the headmen he must go before the general council of the chief society at Rochore, when he will be warned and reproved; if he still prove disobedient, he will be dismissed, and then any trouble he may get into must be borne by himself, as the society will not be responsible.

10.   A member of the Ghi Hok society must above all things honour and obey his parents, if any brother, with evil words, abuse or curse his parents on the headmen being acquainted of it, they will dismiss him from the society.

11.   Any member of the Ghi Hok society (whether headmen or merely a common member) running away with a brother's lawful wife or concubine will be dismissed from the society by the headmen on acquaintance with the fact.

12.   If any member of the Ghi Hok society introduce an offender against the Company's law into the society the headmen knowing of the fact will immediately dismiss such member from the society.

13.   If any member of the Ghi Hok society go abroad and quarrel, wounding or shedding blood, the headmen will not interfere, he must go before the Police and be punished.

14.   On the event of a member of the Ghi Hok society's marriage or if a member to be buried, the brethren should accompany the procession and assist; if a member, after being called twice refuse to come he will be dismissed from the society.

15.   It is not permitted for a member of the Ghi Hok Kongsi to introduce any person employed by the Company into the society, any member of the society introducing a Government employe with will be dismissed from the society.

16.   Any member of the Ghi Hok society being in want of money, and wishing to borrow from another member must deposit jewellery paper or house property as security. The interest must be at the rate of 2 per cent per month and the period three months; if at the end of 3 months the pledge is not redeemed, the lender must give a week's notice, and then if at the expiry of that term the debt is not paid he can sell the goods in pledge by auction for payment.

17. Any member of the Ghi Hok society being arrested by the police for gambling should ask the headmen to bail him out. If he should be sentenced to a fine he must pay for himself as the headmen will have nothing to do with it. If a brother steal from another brother, the headmen after judging the case will dismiss the member from the society.

18. Any member of the Ghi Hok society lending money must conform to the rules of the society as to interest period &c. he must not charge more than two per cent per month.

19. Any member of the Ghi Hok society borrowing or lending property to the amount of 80 or 100 dollars value should first inform the headmen if they do not inform them then in the event of any quarrel, concerning the transaction the headmen will have nothing to do with the matter.

20. If any member of the Ghi Hok society quarrel or fight with wife or child and they run to another member's house, the husband ought to inform the headmen; any member of the society sheltering or hiding another member's wife or child will be dismissed from the society.

21. Any member of the Ghi Hok society being arrested by the police quarrelling or creating disturbance shall apply to headmen to bail him. If the Government sentence him to a fine he must pay it himself as the headmen will have nothing to do with it.

22. The Ghi Hok society have every year two celebrations of the birth days of the 5 ancestors, each member must then subscribe 50 cents, any member twice refusing to subscribe will be dismissed from the society.

23. Any member of the Ghi Hok society cursing abusing or striking his father or mother must be brought before the headmen who will reprove him. If he refuse to listen to the reproofs and orders of the headmen he will be dismissed from the society.

24. If a member of the Ghi Hok society dies and there is not money sufficient for the funeral expenses, on the headmen being acquainted of the fact they will present the sum of $4.

25. Any member of the Ghi Hok society having gone abroad for the purposes of trade, or returned to China. If he should have left wife or child here without means of support on application the headmen will relieve their wants.

26. If any member of the Ghi Hok society is arrested and the headmen on going to bail him out are unsuccessful, that member shall be dismissed from the society.

27. If any member of the Ghi Hok society (having given himself up to gambling prostitutes and such vicious courses) do not return to his house and support his wife and children, the wife or children on application to the headmen will receive the sum of $10 for their support.

28. If any member of the Ghi Hok society away from house and another member come and commit adultery with his wife or child, the headmen on being acquainted with the fact will dismiss the offender from the society.

29. If a member of the Ghi Hok society have a grown up daughter, and other member secretly enter the house and commit adultery with her, the parents on knowing should inform the headmen who will call the offender before them, and order him to marry the girl and to pay $44 to the parents as marriage-money. If he will not obey the advice of the society, the headmen will take the parents to the Police, and assist them to prosecute the offender and he will be dismissed from the society,

30. If any member of the Ghi Hok society by quarrelling and fighting with the members of another Kongsee, offend against the Company's laws, the headmen will admonish and reprove him; if he refuse to listen they will dismiss him from the society and will not be responsible for any trouble he may get into afterwards.

31. The members of the Ghi Hok society should enter into trade and be honest, and labour as coolies &c. they must not go out and create trouble, disturbing the peace and offending against the Company's laws. If any member thus offending be arrested, and his wife or child apply for the headmen to bail him, they will not interfere but will dismiss the member from the society.

32. If any member of the Ghi Hok society have a quarrel with a man, and that man be of the society after his entrance the quarrel must be forgotten. Any member disobeying this rule will not be recognised by the headmen as a member, but will be dismissed from the society.

33. Any member of the Ghi Hok society having sisters or children who are about to marry on application to the headmen he will be presented with the sum of $4.

34. Any member of the Ghi Hok society have a son or daughter about to be married, or if he be about to celebrate his 60th birth day on application to the headmen he will receive the sum of $4.

36. All members of the Ghi Hok society must conform to these 36 rules, and must obey the Company's laws. If they disobey the society's rules or offend against the Company's laws, the headmen will immediately dismiss them from the society.

On entering the Ghi Hok society each member must swear to conform to the above rules and the following is the oath. "If I break any of these rules, may my limbs fall to pieces and may I be turned out of the society and not recognised."

The 36 articles of the oath of the Ghee Hok society.

1. After entering the Hong Gate, a member of the Hong family must above all things obey and honour his parents, he must also abstain from injuring the parents of a brother Hong. If he break this oath may he within 100 days die by being cut to pieces, or in the five seas, his flesh floating on the surface, and his bones sinking to the bottom.

2. After entering the Hong Gate, a member of the Hong family must not relying on his strength oppress the weak he must not favor his relations, the great must not deceive the small. The ancient maxim was "If the son of heaven (Emperor) offend all the people are involved in the guilt. If any brother break this rule may his intestines fall out thunder strike him or fire burn him to death.

3. After entering the Hong Gate, a member of the Hong family must not gamble with a brother or commit lewdness together if he even gamble with a brother, he must not on any account commit lewdness. A brother seeing another brother with money must not try or seek to injure him in order to possess the money. If any brother dare with an evil heart offend against this rule may he within 100 days die under 10,000 knives, his corpse divided and his bones broken; may thunder strike him or fire burn him.

4. After entering the Hong Gate if a brother of the Hong family get into trouble and is arrested by the Government police and is being taken before the magistrate, all Hong brothers must use all their power to interfere and deliver him. If any brother dare disregard this rule and passing the matter over as of no consequence refuse to help to save him may within 100 days thunder strike him down, dead in the road, and his bones perish in the rivers and seas.

5. After entering the Hong Gate, a brother must not for the sake of reward assist in arresting a brother, if any member do so, may he within 100 days die under 10,000 knives.

6. Any member of the Ghi Hok society dying and leaving a wife or children here without means of subsistence if they come and acquaint the headmen they will receive the sum of $1 and 50 catties of white rice.

7. After entering the Hong Gate, a brother whether old or new must conform to the rules, he must not enviously wish to rise to the position of an incense burner. (Heong Choo). In the laws handed down to us the periods are fixed, five years service qualifies him for Hong; ten years for Heong Choo" on the brethren, finding out they will arrest him and punish him with 108 blows and will without fail cut off both his ears.

8. After entering the Hong Gate, a brother must not quarrel and fight with his friend. Each brother has his duties, he has his, you have your's, you must not interfere with him, or commit debauchery with each other. If any member interfere in a disorderly manner or commit debauchery with another brother may the brethren find it out and his naked body perish without mercy.

[121]

9. After entering the Hong Gate, a brother going to visit another brother must eat rice if he have only rice, and conjee, if he have only conjee to offer him he must not complain and be angry with his brother because he has not vegetables to set before him. If any member disregarding this rule should be angry because his brother has no vegetables to offer him, and going about telling other people hurts a brother's good name may be within 100 days die under 10,000 knives and his body fall to pieces.

10. After entering the Hong Gate a brother must not plot against the Heong Choo at the times of ceremonies or theatrical performances, he must not take upon himself to open the door to go in or out not even an inch or a step. If any member dare arrest the Heong Choo or Sein Seng, may on his going abroad, a serpent bite him, a tiger tear him thunder striking or fire burn him may blood flow from his seven holes.

N.B.—The seven holes according to the Chinese, are the eyes, ears, mouth and nostrils.

11. After entering the Hong Gate, a member having taken the pledge of brotherhood, must not use paper and pen to the injury of his brethren. If any brother disregarding this rule use paper and pen to the injury of a brother, may he within 100 days die by the knife or sword.

12. After entering the Hong Gate, if a member see his twin brother (by birth) quarrelling with a Hong brother he ought to interfere and part them. He may try to make peace but must not assist his twin brother against the Hong brother. If any brother disregarding this rule dare assist his brother by birth to fight the brother of Hong within 100 days may five thunders strike him dead may he fall into the rivers or seas his body float on the ocean or fall to pieces.

13. After entering the Hong Gate, if a brother of the Hong family through crime or misfortune is in difficulty and fly to a brother's house, he must be assisted and conducted over the boundaries that he may escape. If a brother disregarding this rule refuse to conduct a Hong brother over the boundaries or to save him may be within 100 days die by the sword and be forgotten.

14. After entering the Hong Gate, a brother of the Hong family must not cheat another brother of money clothes or goods. If any member disregarding this rule dare with an envious heart cheat a brother of money, clothes or goods may be die within 100 days by being cut to pieces or if in the jungle may a tiger devour him.

15. After entering the Hong Gate, if a brother of the Hong family wishing to celebrate the joyful or sorrowful ceremonies of his parents, or if they have arrived at old age and he has no money to use, the whole of the brotherhood must assist him with means. If any brother disregarding this rule should refuse

to assist another brother in such a situation may be die within 100 days by vomiting blood.

16. After entering the Hong Gate, if a brother of a Hong family die and the widow wish to marry again the brethren must not take her for wife. The matter ought to be enquired into, it is not permitted for a Hong brother to marry a brother's widow. From the time of entering the brotherhood the spirits are looking and will notice the least injury to a brother's honour outside people will also sneer and laugh. If any member disregarding this laws of Hong will wed a brother's widow within 100 days may five thunders strike him dead and his body be exposed without burial.

17. After entering the Hong Gate, if a brother of the Hong family see in any place clothes goods or money he must not seal them. If in the country he see grain in the fields he must not himself take it secretly, or get others to forcibly seize it, he ought first ask his brother's permission and then he can take it. If any brother disregarding this rule take without asking his brother's clothes money or goods or if in the country he take grain from the fields the brother on finding it out will punish him with 108 blows and cut off his ears.

18. After entering the Hong Gate, if a man before entering the Hong Gate has killed a parent of a brother and there is a revengeful feeling it must be put away and the brother must not remember the old wrong. If any member dare continue to brood over the injury and desire revenge, may be within 100 days die in the rivers or ocean his flesh floating on the top and bones sinking to the bottom.

19. After entering the Hong Gate, if a brother of the Hong family run away on account of crime, and come into your house to borrow money for expense to escape you must give him the sum necessary, and if there is not sufficient in the house you must give clothes or goods for your brother to pawn that he may have money for his expenses; if any member omit to do his brother's business or refuse to subscribe money to assist and save him, may within one month five thunders strike him dead and his corpse and naked bones perish from the remembrance of men.

20. After entering the Hong Gate on the night of joining and taking pledge of brotherhood a brother of Hong family must not on returning home, secretly dispose of his small jacket, purse, or white clothes, as they are the property of the society a father must not divulge the Hong Laws to his son, or son to his father, an elder brother to a younger brother or a younger brother to an elder. If any brother disregarding this rule thereafter illicitly divulge or teach the Hong Laws, or if he sell privately the society's property, may be within 100 days die by the mouth of tiger or wolf.

21. After entering the Hong Gate, if a brother of the Hong family be entrusted by another brother with letters or money to take home for him, he must use all despatch and deliver the letters and money to the brothers' parents brothers or wife, that they may have the money to use. He must not enviously and unfaithfully detain them. If any member disregarding this rule dare detain or keep a brother's letters or money, may be within 100 days die in the rivers or seas his flesh floating on the top and his bones sinking to the bottom.

22. After entering the Hong Gate a brother of the Hong family must not procure for his own use from his brethren by using false names of by falsely speaking of joyful or sorrowful events. If any brother disregarding this rule dare by such means deceive the brethren and thus get money for his own use may be within 100 days die by the sword.

23. After entering the Hong Gate if a brother borrows money or goods from another brother, it is the duty of proper and honest man if he borrows to return the same, if he does not may he within 100 days hang himself and pigs drag and dogs bite his corpse till it fall to pieces.

24. After entering the Hong Gate a brother of the Hong family must not on account of the number and strength of the brotherhood, contrive and make disturbances judge between right and wrong oppress or impress on the weak, or being strong insult people these things are contrary to the Hong laws. If not listening to the headmen a brother unlawfully insult people &c., within 100 days may he die by poison.

25. After entering the Hong Gate, if a brother of the Hong family be imposed upon by a man he ought to inform the brotherhood in order that they may all come forward and with the strength of their arm assist him. The brethren must come forward to protect and revenge him any brother disregarding this rule and knowing that another brother is being imposed upon does not come forward may be die by the hand of a woman.

26. After entering the Hong Gate, a brother of the Hong family must not boast or exaggerate to another brother or talk carelessly and loosely about things thus injuring the brotherhood by fermenting quarrels and bad feeling. If any brother disregarding this rule dare boast and exaggerate before a brether's face disturb the good feeling of the society may he die by being cut to pieces.

27. After entering the Hong Gate. Brother of the Hong family under heaven these are two capitals and 13 provinces, when a brother visits your house, you must immediately welcome him with tea and rice (food) you must not send him away angrily or refuse to receive him. If any (brother) member disregarding this rule dare angrily refuse to receive or entertain a brother, may be die by his seven holes flowing with blood and his corpse for ever fall to pieces.

28. After entering the Hong Gate. Brethren of the Hong family must not gather together and walk abroad in threes or fives creating disturbances and injuring the brotherhood; the ancient maxim is let each attend to his proper trade or occupation and do not mix with evil business, wait till the rebellion and disorder is over and the day of the obedience to the Ming dynasty has arrived the Manchoos are all slain and our protector Lord ascends the throne. He will appoint us to offices and confer nobility upon us then the patriotic and generous reputation of the Hong brotherhood will be established. If any brother disregarding the commands and instructions of the brethren should act tumultously or create disturbance thus injuring the (reputation of) brotherhood may be die and his intestines fall out.

29. After entering the Hong Gate. On receiving the orders from the 2 capitals and 13 Provinces of the world (China) the brethren must gather the Hong, and assemble the soldiers, call the Council together to examine the orders of the two Capitals and 13 Provinces and not divulge them; if he does may he die by being cut to pieces or in the five seas.

30. After entering the Hong Gate. If a person who has formerly acted as an informer and assisted to arrest a Hong brother should wish to enter the society members should inform the brethren that they may come forward arrest and hand him over to the council for punishment they must not let him escape. If a brother through friendship with the man's society favour his escape may he die under 1000 knives.

31. After entering the Hong Gate a brother of the Hong family going abroad for the purposes of trade or business, and being ignorant of the affairs of his house by reason of distance, if his wife or child commit evil with any man a brother knowing of it must inform the brethren that they may come forward and arrest the offending man and thus uphold the generous and honest reputation of the Hong family. If any brother disregarding this rule and knowing of such things do not call the brethren to come forward and arrest the offender may he be drowned in the rivers and oceans.

32. After entering the Hong Gate a brother of the Hong family dying and leaving a wife and children if the widow remain chaste, and any outside people wish to oppress them or rob them of fields, gardens, house or property they ought to inform the brethren in order that they may come forward, and protect the widow of the Hong family and recover her fields houses or property, so that the wife and children may be fed. We must remember our sworn brother and hand down our great reputation to 10,000 generation. If any member wilfully disregarding this rule do not call the brethren to come forward and protect a brother's widow with their strength may be die where three roads meet may five thunders strike him dead fire burn him and his seven holes flow with blood.

33. After entering the Hong Gate. The laws handed down from the five ancestors all inculcate obedience to parents and forbid disobedience. If any brother listening to wife or concubine dare disobey or neglect his parents, may he die by 1,000 or 10,000 knives.

34. After entering the Hong Gate, a new brother of Hong on the night of instalment, must with a true heart before Heaven draw blood and take the important oath of friendship. He must on returning home under a tree at the head of the street, or the end of a lane, or in a shrine or temple repeat this vow. The spirits are beholding and regarding the oath taken this night before heaven, any man dares with a false heart take the oath may he die on the road thunder strike or fire burn him.

35. After entering the Hong Gate, a brother of the Hong family having on this night sincerely sworn to these things he must know that sincerity and filial obedience are above all things; if a brother commit wife or child to his care he must follow the example of the ancients Tek Tee, Peng-Tai-Hong-Tay-chan and Lee Sek-Khan, then he will have reputation for sincerity and virtue for 10,000 generations. If any brother cannot be trusted with another brother's wife or child, may he within 100 days die by blood flowing from his seven holes.

36. After entering the Hong Gate a brother of the Hong family on this night of taking the oath (must know) that the spirits are regarding and our five ancestors when first establishing the Golden Brotherhood arranged these oaths which have been handed down till now, all the brethren must mutually fulfil them, and sincerely and virtuously walk according to them. They must not disregard the oath. If any brother with a false heart take the vow, and afterwards does insincere and dishonorable things, may he die by 1,000 knives and 10,000 spears, and may an arrow secretly strike him. If with a sincere heart you obey and walk according to the oaths, then you will have 10,000 happiness and felicities.

THE END

Some other Oxford Paperbacks for readers interested in Central Asia, China, Japan, and South-East Asia, past and present

Cambodia

GEORGE COEDÈS
Angkor

MALCOLM MacDONALD
Angkor and the Khmers*

Central Asia

PETER FLEMING
Bayonets to Lhasa

ANDRÉ GUIBAUT
Tibetan Venture

LADY MACARTNEY
An English Lady in Chinese Turkestan

DIANA SHIPTON
The Antique Land

C. P. SKRINE AND
PAMELA NIGHTINGALE
Macartney at Kashgar*

ERIC TEICHMAN
Journey to Turkistan

ALBERT VON LE COQ
Buried Treasures of Chinese Turkestan

AITCHEN K. WU
Turkistan Tumult

China

All About Shanghai: A Standard Guide

L. C. ARLINGTON AND WILLIAM LEWISOHN
In Search of Old Peking

VICKI BAUM
Shanghai '37

ERNEST BRAMAH
Kai Lung's Golden Hours*

ERNEST BRAMAH
The Wallet of Kai Lung*

ANN BRIDGE
The Ginger Griffin

NIGEL CAMERON
The Chinese Smile

CHANG HSIN-HAI
The Fabulous Concubine*

CARL CROW
Handbook for China

PETER FLEMING
The Siege at Peking

ROBERT FORD
Captured in Tibet

MARY HOOKER
Behind the Scenes in Peking

NEALE HUNTER
Shanghai Journal*

GEORGE N. KATES
The Years that Were Fat

CORRINNE LAMB
The Chinese Festive Board

ALEKO LILIUS
I Sailed with Chinese Pirates

G. E. MORRISON
An Australian in China

DESMOND NEILL
Elegant Flower

PETER QUENNELL
A Superficial Journey through Tokyo and Peking

OSBERT SITWELL
Escape with Me! An Oriental Sketchbook

J. A. TURNER
Kwang Tung or Five Years in South China

JULES VERNE
The Tribulations of a Chinese Gentleman

Hong Kong and Macau

AUSTIN COATES
City of Broken Promises

AUSTIN COATES
A Macao Narrative

AUSTIN COATES
Macao and the British, 1637–1842

AUSTIN COATES
Myself a Mandarin

AUSTIN COATES
The Road

The Hong Kong Guide 1893

Indonesia

VICKI BAUM
A Tale from Bali*

'BENGAL CIVILIAN'
Rambles in Java and the Straits in 1852

VIOLET CLIFTON
Islands of Indonesia

MIGUEL COVARRUBIAS
Island of Bali*

AUGUSTA DE WIT
Java: Facts and Fancies

JACQUES DUMARÇAY
The Temples of Java

ANNA FORBES
Unbeaten Tracks in Islands of the Far East

HAROLD FORSTER
Flowering Lotus: A View of Java in the 1950s

GEOFFREY GORER
Bali and Angkor

JENNIFER LINDSAY
Javanese Gamelan

EDWIN M. LOEB
Sumatra: Its History and People

MOCHTAR LUBIS
Indonesia: Land under the Rainbow

MOCHTAR LUBIS
The Outlaw and Other Stories

MOCHTAR LUBIS
Twilight in Djakarta

MADELON H. LULOFS
Coolie

MADELON H. LULOFS
Rubber

COLIN McPHEE
A House in Bali*

H. W. PONDER
Java Pageant

H. W. PONDER
Javanese Panorama

JAN POORTENAAR
An Artist in Java and Other Islands of Indonesia

HICKMAN POWELL
The Last Paradise

F. M. SCHNITGER
Forgotten Kingdoms in Sumatra

E. R. SCIDMORE
Java, The Garden of the East

MICHAEL SMITHIES
Yogyakarta: Cultural Heart of Indonesia

LADISLAO SZÉKELY
Tropic Fever: The Adventures of a Planter in Sumatra

ALFRED RUSSEL WALLACE
The Malay Archipelago

HARRY WILCOX
Six Moons in Sulawesi

Japan

WILLIAM PLOMER
Sado

Malaysia

ODOARDO BECCARI
Wanderings in the Great Forests of Borneo

ISABELLA L. BIRD
The Golden Chersonese: Travels in Malaya in 1879

CARL BOCK
The Head-Hunters of Borneo

MARGARET BROOKE
THE RANEE OF SARAWAK
My Life in Sarawak

SYLVIA, LADY BROOKE
THE RANEE OF SARAWAK
Queen of the Head-hunters

F. W. BURBIDGE
The Gardens of the Sun

SIR HUGH CLIFFORD
Saleh: A Prince of Malaya

IVOR H. N. EVANS
Among Primitive Peoples in Borneo

HENRI FAUCONNIER
The Soul of Malaya

C. W. HARRISON
Illustrated Guide to the Federated Malay States (1923)

BARBARA HARRISSON
Orang-Utan

TOM HARRISSON
Borneo Jungle

TOM HARRISSON
World Within: A Borneo Story

CHARLES HOSE
Natural Man

W. SOMERSET MAUGHAM
Ah King and Other Stories*

W. SOMERSET MAUGHAM
The Casuarina Tree*

ROBERT PAYNE
The White Rajahs of Sarawak

Philippines

LEON WOLFF
Little Brown Brother

Singapore

RUSSELL GRENFELL
Main Fleet to Singapore

MASANOBU TSUJI
Singapore 1941–1942

C. W. WURTZBURG
Raffles of the Eastern Isles

Thailand

CARL BOCK
Temples and Elephants

ANNA LEONOWENS
The English Governess at the Siamese Court

SIBURAPHA
Behind the Painting and Other Stories

MALCOLM SMITH
A Physician at the Court of Siam

ERNEST YOUNG
The Kingdom of the Yellow Robe

* Titles marked with an asterisk have restricted rights.